POSSESSING THE GATES OF THE ENEMY

Strategic Spiritual Warfare Manual

DR. GEORGE AGBONSON

Christ Restoration Publications

Possessing The Gates of The Enemy
Dr. George Agbonson
Copyright © 2013 by Christ Restoration Publications
ISBN: 978-0-6157-9345-0

Christ Restoration Publications
740 Lakeview Plaza Blvd. Unit 325
Worthington, OH 43085
www.christrestoration.net

Printed in the United States of America

*Scripture text in bold is the emphasis of the author.

TABLE OF CONTENT

INTRODUCTION..x
PART ONE: KINGDOM WARFARE..........................[12]
CHAPTER ONE: TWO KINGDOMS AT WAR.................[13]
CHAPTER TWO: THE BATTLE IS AT THE GATE.............[21]
CHAPTER THREE: SPIRITUAL SIGNIFICANCE OF THE
GATE...[25]

**PART TWO: NEHEMIAH'S PROJECT OF
RESTORATION**
CHAPTER ONE: CATCH THE VISION.......................[32]
CHAPTER TWO: RESTORATION BEGINS AT THE GATE[39]
CHAPTER THREE: WATCHMEN ON THE WALL..........[74]

PART THREE: PULLING DOWN ANCIENT GATES
INTRODUCTION....................................[82]
CHAPTER ONE: MARINE POWERS........................[86]
CHAPTER TWO: SERPENTINE POWERS...................[92]
CHAPTER THREE: WITCHCRAFT POWERS...............[97]
CHAPTER FOUR: OCCULT POWERS IN HIGH PLACES.[101]

PART FOUR: LET THE CHURCH ARISE
INTRODUCTION..[113]
CHAPTER ONE: I WILL BUILD MY CHURCH.............[115]
CHAPTER TWO: AUTHORITY OF THE CHURCH.........[123]

ENDORSEMENTS

It is with great honor that I am privileged to endorse this book. Apostle George Agbonson, my son in the Gospel has written this book with such precise timing. Being the founder of Gap Closers Church International *"Repairers of the Breach"* and the *"Gatekeepers"* Prayer Ministry, I have a full mandate and understanding of spiritual warfare and possessing the gates! I challenge every leader and believer to embrace the pages of this book as it is truly a strategic weapon for the Body of Christ. You will learn the keys to the Kingdom of Heaven and how to walk in power and authority. The Kingdom of God will advance and the world will be forever impacted as the Elijah's of God, arise!

Apostle Dr. Veronica A. Johnson
Gap Closers Church International,
Decatur, AL/Las Vegas, NV

This book is a weapon that will help defeat the enemy. It's a wake up for the body of Christ. As you read this book you will be able to stand on " no weapon form against me shall prosper ". I endorse this work by my brother and friend Apostle George Agbonson

Apostle Dr. Frederick Gelsey
Founder/Senior Pastor
One In Christ Temple
Buffalo, NY

This dynamic Spiritual Warfare Manual from Dr. George Agbonson is a clarion call for all those who sense a call to be End-Time Reformers like Nehemiah. He makes a bold but true statement that "whoever possesses the gates also possesses the destiny of a region". It is time for you and me to "put on the whole armor of God" and repossess the gates of our cities and nation(s) through strategic spiritual warfare and evangelism. This book delivers the necessary tools to accomplish just that. Highly recommended!

Alfred Tagoe

Founder, Voice of Revival Ministries

Columbus, OH

INTRODUCTION

The question of where evil began has been debated all through history. The simple truth is that it all began in Heaven. Lucifer was an arch-angel who was adored by all angels. He beheld the face of God every morning. He was the worship angel; full of splendor, beauty and power until the day evil was conceived in him. He was a special kind of angel. God created Lucifer specially. He wasn't just an angel but an arch-angel; a lead angel.

You were the anointed cherub who covers; I established you; You were on the holy mountain of God; You walked back and forth in the midst of fiery stones. You were perfect in your ways from the day you were created, Till iniquity was found in you. "By the abundance of your trading You became filled with violence within, And you sinned; Therefore I cast you as a profane thing Out of the mountain of God; And I destroyed you, O covering cherub, From the midst of the fiery stones. "Your heart was lifted up because of your beauty; You corrupted your wisdom for the sake of your splendor; I cast you to the ground, I laid you before kings, That they might gaze at you. "You defiled your sanctuaries By the multitude of your iniquities, By the iniquity of your trading; Therefore I brought fire from your midst; It devoured you, And I turned you to ashes upon the earth In the sight of all who saw you. All who knew you among the peoples are astonished at you; You have become a horror, And shall be no more forever. Ezekiel 28:14-19

Little would anyone believe that the evil acts of Lucifer who later became the Devil would metamorphose? It was the beginning of what every generation will battle for the rest of humanity until the culmination of the age. Lucifer's downfall came as a result of pride… wanting to be equal with God or (better said,) placed side by side with God. He was unsatisfied with where he was. Lucifer wanted more adoration, worship and above all; he wanted to be in control. However, in the end he got the opposite. Instead of exaltation he was expelled from heaven and was sentenced to everlasting damnation.

How you are fallen from heaven, O Lucifer, son of the morning! How you are cut down to the ground, You who weakened the nations! **For you have said in your heart: 'I will ascend into heaven, I will** *exalt my throne above the stars of God; I will also sit on the mount of the congregation On the farthest sides of the north; I will ascend above the heights of the clouds, I will be like the Most High.' Yet you shall be brought down to Sheol, To the lowest depths of the Pit. "Those who see you will gaze at you, And consider you, saying: 'Is this the man who made the earth tremble, Who shook kingdoms, Who made the world as a wilderness And destroyed its cities, Who did not open the house of his prisoners?'* Isaiah 14:12-17

This ended the service of the arch-angel Lucifer in heaven amongst other angels, but it was the beginning of what we call today, *'Spiritual Warfare'*. His name changed from Lucifer to Satan or the Devil.

To deny the existence of the Devil today will mean to disbelieve the Bible. To deny the power of the Devil is to be ignorant of how angelic beings were made. We cannot underestimate him. Nowhere in the Bible are we told that God stripped him of his power, beauty, splendor, knowledge, etc. *The only thing that changed about Lucifer was his purpose. Do not underestimate his power, don't be fooled.* The change in his purpose from good to evil channeled everything in him towards destruction. This is

9

the starting point in understanding spiritual warfare. There is nothing good about the Devil. To pity him is to destroy your own destiny. He can never be changed, never be transformed or delivered. He is doomed for everlasting destruction.

The purpose of this book therefore, is to teach you how to fight this Devil strategically. We have too many fighters in the Kingdom, but too many naive fighters. Many Christians are losing the battle by the day yet claim to have victory in Christ. The church is losing its ground to the enemy yet it claims to be possessing territories for Christ. Who is deceiving who? You only know what a tree is by the fruits it bears not what it looks like.

> We have learnt about spiritual warfare, the Devil, and Demons. But many still don't know *"How to fight"*.

We have learnt about spiritual warfare, the Devil, and Demons. But many still don't know *"How to fight."* This book is not about teaching people about the Devil. We've heard that enough. Now, it is time to learn how to bring this Devil under our feet where he belongs by learning how to be a strategic fighter. No longer will you waste your sweat anymore. You will hit the bull eye the next time you shoot. If you don't put the Devil where he belongs, he will place himself where he wants to be which is to rule your life and destiny. It is high time to determine who will take charge of our lives, our cities, nation, government, education, business, family, media, churches, etc. Are you ready to become a strategic fighter?

PART ONE

KINGDOM WARFARE

CHAPTER ONE

TWO KINGDOMS AT WAR

*And war broke out in heaven: Michael and his angels fought with the dragon; and the dragon and his angels fought, but **they did not prevail, nor was a place found for them in heaven any longer**. So the great dragon was cast out, that serpent of old, called the Devil and Satan, who deceives the whole world; he was cast to the earth, and his angels were cast out with him. Then I heard a loud voice saying in heaven, "Now salvation, and strength, and the kingdom of our God, and the power of His Christ have come, for the accuser of our brethren, who accused them before our God day and night, has been cast down. And they overcame him by the blood of the Lamb and by the word of their testimony, and they did not love their lives to the death. **Therefore rejoice, O heavens, and you who dwell in them! Woe to the inhabitants of the earth and the sea! For the devil has come down to you, having great wrath,** because he knows that he has a short time."* Revelation 12:7-12

There are two opposing kingdoms in existence: The Kingdom of God and the Kingdom of Satan - The Kingdom of Light and the Kingdom of Darkness and everyone on Earth belong to one or the other. Every Born Again Christian belongs to the Kingdom of God and is automatically enlisted for war. That's right! War.

It is not a matter of choice but a matter of destiny. This war started in heaven like it is highlighted in the above scripture. The Devil did not only lose the battle in heaven; He was cast out of there. He has no position in heaven anymore. Now the greatest tragedy is that he didn't fall from heaven smiling, laughing or partying. He fell down defeated. Have you ever seen a football team defeated before? Do they celebrate? *The Devil came down in rage.* Not him alone but a company of fallen angels who became demons. Now, you'll understand why the Bible says *'Woe'* to those who live on earth. It means war. The battle is between Light and Darkness about who controls the world? The Devil is with us here on earth not with God in heaven. Like Francis Frangipane asserts:

Many Christians debate whether the devil is on earth or in hell; can he dwell in Christians or only in the world? The fact is; the devil is in darkness. Where there is spiritual darkness, there the devil will be. The devil and the fallen angels with him have been relegated to live in darkness. This darkness does not simply refer to areas void of visible light. Satan has a legal access, given to him by God, to dwell in the domain of darkness. The devil can traffic in any area of darkness.[1]

I believe ignorance is one of the greatest diseases that many Christian suffer from. Those who should know or claim to be knowledgeable in Scripture have half-baked knowledge in this area of spiritual warfare. So Christians end up learning the extreme version of faith which claims that Satan is totally powerless and defeated, therefore, we don't need to fight anymore. The question now is why is he still here? Why do we still have the kingdom of darkness operating in our families, cities, nation, education, church, government, business? One who is defeated should not have a place to occupy anymore. The above scripture again says not only was the Devil defeated in heaven, he was also cast out. He has no place anymore. Meaning he has no control whatsoever. This is why God has you reading this book. Your mindset is about to change about spiritual warfare.

The truth is that the Devil came down to earth like we read with his kingdom of demons to occupy the darkness. They established several sub-kingdom groups within the realm of darkness since he had a lot of demons with him. Kingdoms of darkness in the air, on the earth, under the earth, and in the Sea. These Kingdoms also comprises of heads over groups or regions known as Principalities. These are one of the major demons we wrestle against.

Warfare is a craft

My other book: *"Deliverance by Fire"* will teach you how to bombard these kingdoms, the devil and his demons with prayers. These Satanic kingdoms were established to ruin mankind, oppose God's will for mankind before Jesus Christ came to redeem us. Thus, you can deduce that Satan is a strategic and organized fighter. He learned a lot in heaven as an arch-angel. He understood the importance of a hierarchical system as a result of what he was privy to or witnessed in heaven. Above all he knows he does not possess the omnipresence quality of God. So the only way he can run his mission is to be very organized and strategic. If only the Body of Christ would come to the realization of his devices we will stop throwing prayer points in the air in vain; tearing our vocal chords apart and screaming only to experience no result. It is time to redefine spiritual warfare. We need to fight strategically. Satan is very crafty. Think about it: how could He run a kingdom if he is stupid? *Warfare is a craft.* You have to learn the art to be skillful in it.

From the beginning of creation, the Devil has been attempting to perpetuate the destruction of mankind. We saw his first manifestation against mankind in the Garden of Eden, (Genesis 3). He succeeded in defeating mankind out of God's will. That is what He is still busy doing. His assignment is well spelled out. John 10:10 says: *"The thief does not come except to steal, and to kill, and to destroy."*

Jesus knew what He meant when He made the statement: *"And from the days of John the Baptist until now the kingdom of heaven suffers violence, and the violent take it by force."* John 11:12

John the Baptist was the fore-runner of Jesus. He came to prepare the way for the King. Jesus' coming was to inaugurate a new Kingdom. John the Baptist was a herald. He was an announcer. He proclaimed to all that a new Kingdom was on its way. John wasn't talking about a Kingdom the world had seen which only promoted the oppression and darkness under Satan's Reign; but he was speaking of the Kingdom of Light which was coming to overthrow the darkness. Have you ever seen a King without

17

a Kingdom? Jesus was proclaimed King of which Kingdom? He brought the Kingdom of God to men and His purpose was to deliver us from darkness. This correlates with His message of salvation. This Kingdom of Light could not be established without uprooting the existing Kingdom of Darkness.

> *But if I cast out demons with the finger of God, surely **the kingdom of God has come upon you**. When a strong man, fully armed, guards his own palace, his goods are in peace. But when a stronger than he comes upon him and overcomes him, he takes from him all his armor in which he trusted, and divides his spoils.* Luke 11:20-22

Satan doesn't give up easily without a fight. This was what Jesus meant when He said it will take force and power to subdue the enemy which He did finally on the cross. All through His ministry, He exhibited the Kingdom of God in Power over the Kingdom of Darkness by delivering people from oppression; bondages of the Devil; healing sicknesses; forgiving many of their sins, etc. Those displays were the fruit of the Kingdom of God over Darkness. Now, the Kingdom of God has been inaugurated.

The citizens of this Kingdom are the Christians who live within it. So when the people are still oppressed by the Devil, where is the Kingdom of God in demonstration? Kingdom is about rule and reign. It's about authority and power, it's about lifestyle. Jesus has committed the keys of the Kingdom of God to us so we are to continue its expansion and advancement by uprooting darkness out of the way; delivering others from the shackles of darkness.

Satan understands this plan now so he is fighting anyone that bears the name of Jesus. His wrath is doubled against Christians because he felt deceived by the crucifixion. *"But we speak the wisdom of God in a mystery, the hidden wisdom which God ordained before the ages for our glory, which none of the rulers of this age knew; for had they known, they would not have crucified the Lord of glory."* 1 Corinthians 2:8

If he had known he wouldn't have crucified Jesus. Now he is turned to you as a Christian because he knows his time is short. That was the whole essence of Revelation 12:7-12. It is apocalyptic in nature yet concealed in history. Now, do you believe you are at war? Do you see the reason why the battle never seems to end? Yet the battle is won if we know how to make the Devil subject to us and put him where he belongs by utilizing strategic prayers of warfare by faith. I am not talking about using simple confessions as though in a theological debate but I am speaking of exercising kingdom dominion as our Lord Jesus did.

CHAPTER TWO

THE BATTLE BEGINS AT THE GATE

> *'Whoever controls the*
> *gates controls the city.'*

We have learnt so far about fighting spiritual battles strategically. One major thrust of this book will be to teach people the importance of gates in spiritual warfare. We will emphasize more in this area as we proceed throughout the pages of the book. *'Spiritual Gate'* is one aspect I believe has not been well taught in spiritual warfare. The truth about kingdom warfare is that *'whoever controls the gates controls the city.'*

I intend to unveil this mystery in this book, that it is time for the battle to be taken back to the most crucial place in warfare. The gate of a house, city or nation is so important to the safety, and progress of the people. In America you hear the talk about national security a lot, why? After what happened on September 11, 2001, The United States of America has never been the same. Ever since then, security in this country has been beefed up so much that no President will be elected if he does not have plans for our military or plans to strengthen our international borders because the borders are the physical gates to America. Whoever is in charge of the border will eventually affect the whole country. One of the biggest crimes America has been fighting for years now is drug trafficking. Trafficking drugs has not only corrupted the nation but it has destroyed a lot of people by killing their dreams and eventually taking their lives, etc. Most of the times these drug crimes creep in from foreign soil through the gates, and the effect become obvious to the whole country. Please read the article below from the New York Times about the U.S border (gate):

Drug traffickers have long profited here and in other Texas border towns. **But their success has sometimes depended on forging unusual alliances.** *Some of the very officers sworn to combat the drug trade have been illicitly earning cash by helping vehicles transporting marijuana and cocaine avoid detection from law enforcement agents, serving as escorts and scouts during the shipments, the authorities say. Last month, four lawmen — two Hidalgo County sheriff's deputies and two Mission police officers — were arrested and accused of escorting loads of drugs in exchange for cash after a corruption investigation led by the Drug Enforcement Administration, the F.B.I. and other*

22

agencies. In court documents filed by federal investigators, the four men were accused of escorting vehicles carrying cocaine for $2,000 to $6,000 per trip.[2]

The Reporter stated in his findings that those who should be guarding the gates were actually the ones perpetuating the crimes. The article continued to say:

> *They were not ordinary patrolmen. Officials said they were part of a task force called the Panama Unit that was formed to fight drug trafficking in Hidalgo County, part of the South Texas border region known as the Rio Grande Valley. **Each had been a licensed peace officer** for five to seven years and had received specialized training in investigative techniques and firearms.*[3]

The above scenarios buttress the point that whoever controls the gates controls whatever happens within. This is just the physical gate to America as a country, now imagine the spiritual gates. Who is in charge?

Most highways in America have an entrance and exit ramp. Most buildings have an entrance and exit door. So, also the life of every individual, there are always two doors or gates to life; entrance and exit - birth and death. There is a spiritual gate to every family, every marriage, every life, to every village, city, nation, organization, and

23

business. The battle we fight today within is as a result of what happens at our gates. Let's take it back there and you will be amazed of the unprecedented victory you will witness. I decree henceforth, that you will begin to take charge of your gates in the Name of Jesus!

CHAPTER THREE

SPIRITUAL SIGNIFICANCE OF GATES

*"Blessing I will bless you, and multiplying I will multiply your descendants as the stars of the heaven and as the sand which is on the seashore; **and your descendants shall possess the gate of their enemies.**"* Gen. 22:17

The third blessing pronounced on Abraham as highlighted above was that his descendants will possess the gate of their enemies. That was very prophetic. God knew exactly what He meant by that statement. You cannot increase, expand, and enlarge your territory without conquering. You cannot conquer a territory without possessing the gates. The gate is the entrance point. Could it be the reason why the children of Israel experienced lots of victory in their conquest of Canaan? The children of Israel had to go through a major gate called Jericho in order to possess their blessing. Jericho was one strategic places in history. The direction to Canaan was through Jericho. They met a huge wall… big gigantic gate standing between them and their promise land. There was no way of reaching their destination without possessing that gate or pulling down the walls. Jericho was a place known for its defense - 'High Walls' with gates. Historians reveal that the walls were so large that the soldiers literally rode horses on them to guard the city from attack.

As a result of God's faithfulness to his promise, the walls of Jericho came down and the children of God possessed the gate, and took over the city (Joshua 6). Look at what Joshua the warrior said after they possessed the gate: *"Then Joshua charged them at that time, saying, "Cursed be the man before the LORD who rises up and builds this city Jericho; he shall lay its foundation with his firstborn, and **with his youngest he shall set up its gates.**"* Joshua 6:26

> *Until you conquer at the gate you will not become significant.*

Joshua indeed knew the significance of gates. Many today are working hard, running with their prophetic words, un-manifested blessings, great anointing, dreams, visions and ideas but wonder why they are not making it. ***Until you conquer at the gate you will not become significant.***

There was another case of a prophetic word given by the prophet Elisha that was battled at the gate: *"Then*

Elisha said, "Hear the word of the LORD. Thus says the LORD: 'Tomorrow about this time a seah of fine flour shall be sold for a shekel, and two seahs of barley for a shekel, at the gate of Samaria." 2 Kings 7:1

There was economic hardship at this time; a national crisis. You see at that time they knew what the anointing was capable of. The anointing can lock and unlock. Elijah did it before Elisha came on the scene so the people knew the power of the anointing unlike many today because although they are anointed they don't know the magnitude of power that God has given to them. Many of the people who do know the power of the anointing, experience a lack of understanding on how and where to channel the anointing. Listen! That is why God has you reading this book. Please pay close attention.

Like Elijah, Elisha was a strategic warrior as well. He knew that the gate to the Economy of the nation had been captured by a Principality. He spoke the Word to the gate of the nation's finance. Although it seemed impossible, that one of the King's adviser who could probably be likened to the Secretary of the Treasury, or Finance Minister of today doubted and ridiculed the prophecy because he lacked spiritual understanding of the gates. He thought it was an ordinary disaster, not knowing that nothing happens in the natural without emanating from the spirit realm. On account of his ridicule, the war at the gate claimed his life:

> *Now the king had appointed the officer on whose hand he leaned to have charge of the gate. But the people trampled him in the gate, and he died, just as the man of God had said, who spoke when the king came down to him. So it happened just as the man of God had spoken to the king, saying, "Two seahs of barley for a shekel, and a seah of fine flour for a shekel, shall be sold tomorrow about this time in the gate of Samaria."* 2 Kings 7:17-18

Please never take the issue of spiritual gates lightly. It has serious implications. Gates are very symbolic. All throughout scripture you will see it referenced, why? Whoever controls the gate controls the people's destiny.

There are key spiritual truths that must be understood on the significance of gates in the Bible that will further aid your study as we proceed. It is certain that the major players and key figures in the Old Testament truly understood the significance of gates in their generation which contributed to their exploit.

IMPORTANCE OF GATES IN THE OLD TESTAMENT:

1. Economic Gate: It was a place of legal business transaction. The gate was a busy place with people going in and out of the city. It was the best place to makes sales. (2 Kings 7:1; Ruth 4:1)

2. Government Gate: It was a place to execute justice. Kings met with people there to settle disputes, and legal matters. (Jer. 38:7)

3. Media Gate: It was a place to herald news. A place for public speaking. The quickest ways for news to travel far was by going to the gate. (Jer. 17:19-20)

4. Religious Gate: It was a place where the Word of the Lord was preached. (2 Chron. 32:6-8). This gate also served as a place of education because the religion of Israel and their education was intertwined. Please note that even the temples had gates.

5. City Gate: The strength of the city or nation was known by their gate. It represented a symbol of strength or weakness. (Joshua 6)

6. Family Gate: No one could enter a house without going through the door or gate; not even angels or demons. (Gen.18:1-2; Ex.12:7)

These are just a few among many gates represented in the Bible. They are very significant. Now you see the reason why many Christians are living a defeated life. Today, this revelation has being placed in your hands. You will start channeling your prayers first to the gates before any other places or concerns. When you know how to pray strategically you will see results.

My other book: *"Deliverance By Fire"* is a practical prayer book that aligns with what you are studying now. Please take time to address the gate that controls whichever area that you've been having issues or problems. Arrest that gate now in the Name of Jesus. There is still more to learn just keep reading.

PART TWO

NEHEMIAH'S PROJECT OF RESTORATION

CHAPTER ONE

CATCH THE VISION

It came to pass in the month of Chislev, in the twentieth year, as I was in Shushan the citadel, that Hanani one of my brethren came with men from Judah; and I asked them concerning the Jews who had escaped, who had survived the captivity, and concerning Jerusalem. And they said to me, "The survivors who are left from the captivity in the province are there in great distress and reproach. ***The wall of Jerusalem is also broken down, and its gates are burned with fire."*** *So it was, when I heard these words, that I sat down and wept, and mourned for many days; I was fasting and praying before the God of heaven. Nehemiah 1:1-4*

The Book of Nehemiah actually depicts and explores the plan of God in the rebuilding of God's kingdom on earth. The book deals with the restoration of mankind to His original intent for dominion, possession and representation of God on earth. This book is a catalyst for the revival that has been prophesied which I believe will manifest in our generation.

God never leaves us in the dark. He always provides the blue print or plan for whatever move that will be birth on earth. Nehemiah happens to be that one Prophet with the anointing for restoration and reformation. He was a strategic fighter. He knew how to conquer and repossess. There is no better person to learn from than this great man of God; Nehemiah.

Anytime God intends to unleash a Kingdom move or a revival, He always sought for kingdom minded individuals. Nehemiah happened to be such a man. He was a kingdom minded minister. He knew what it meant to be in power or a position of influence. The story of Nehemiah began by letting us know that this man occupied a sensitive position in the Babylonian kingdom. He was a cupbearer.

> *"And it came to pass in the month of Nisan, in the twentieth year of King Artaxerxes, when wine was before him, that I took the wine and gave it to the king."* Neh. 2:1

The office of a cupbearer is a sensitive one, he not only serves the King drinks but taste the drink before it is served. The life of the King is practically in the hands of the cupbearer. If the King will be poisoned it must go through the cupbearer. So Nehemiah had to be trusted for such a sensitive and dangerous position. He definitely knew what governance of a kingdom was because of his position. The cupbearer has to be available when the King is having several meetings especially political and leadership meetings. Most political matters were discussed over a cup of wine. Nehemiah knew what it felt like to rule from the High Place indeed. On account of serving the King, he knew that when the unrighteous are in power, the people suffer.

God did not make a mistake about choosing him at all. He was definitely the right man for the job. He had been in the High Place of power. Like Nehemiah, there are people today God has strategically positioned in places of power and influence. As we study, I believe the hearts of many will be ignited (just as it happened to Nehemiah,) for this end time revival.

God is looking for people like Nehemiah who understands that the broken walls and destruction of the gates of Jerusalem means that the Devil is in charge and that the people will experience nothing but oppression from the Devil's satanic agendas which he promotes. If these horrific agendas are not destroyed, then the futures of our children are in jeopardy. Just like it happened in the days of Nehemiah so it is today. *The broken down walls of our day represents the prayerlessness of the Body of Christ and the burnt gate is the dominion that has been lost to the Devil.*

What happened in the days of Nehemiah is a type or a shadow of what is going on in the Body of Christ and the world at large today. Remember what we have learnt so far, whoever controls the gate controls the people as well.

Nehemiah didn't feel comfortable. He had a good job, good career, good position and a good life at the palace. Yet, he knew that his purpose for being positioned in the house of the King went beyond all of the good things that he was experiencing daily. He knew his faith in God was jeopardized if his spiritual covering was gone. Do you understand where his brokenness came from when he asked about Jerusalem?

> *And they said to me, "The survivors who are left from the captivity in the province are there in great distress and reproach. The wall of Jerusalem is also broken down, and its gates are burned with fire. So it was, when I heard these words that I sat down and wept, and mourned for many days; I was*

fasting and praying before the God of heaven. Neh. 1:3-4

Do you know that the broken walls and burnt gates meant that there was no more covering for the covenant children of God? When there is no covering, your life is constantly in danger. Do you know why we are experiencing increase of evil in our cities and nations? It's because the spiritual walls are broken and the spiritual gates have been captured by the enemy. When a wall of a house goes down, anything is allowed to creep into that house. And when the gate of a house is destroyed it literally means the protection of that home is gone. People can't live comfortably there anymore. Where are the spiritual walls and gates of America today? You know the answer.

Why do most Christian parent refuse want to send their children to public schools anymore? Why is there so much shooting going on in the schools today? Our public schools are no longer safe physically, psychologically, intellectually and spiritually. This is the result of taking Bibles out of the school system. Prayers were abolished as well. The walls were broken down and the enemy captured the gates of our educational system. Now we see the fruit thereof.

Definitely, Congress passed the law to abolished Bibles and prayers from schools which of course were Satan's agenda. Where were the Daniels, Josephs, and Esther in the Senate? Probably they fought but didn't have enough support. Besides support, they lacked spiritual understanding, thereby giving the education gate to the Devil. *"For we do not wrestle against flesh and blood, but against principalities, against powers, against the rulers of the darkness of this age, against spiritual hosts of wickedness in the heavenly places."* Eph. 6:12

Rather than contending against the Principality which intends to seize the education gate, many were busy fighting on paper and with endless arguments of words that leads to nowhere. Again, this is where the Church at large was supposed to come in. While the Daniels in the High Places like the Senate were busy contending against the bill, the Body of Christ should have been busy praying and strategically casting out every Demon infiltrating the Senate and school system. This is just one gate we are looking at, the education gate, let alone the economic gate, the political gate, the media gate, etc. Now you see why we need the Nehemiah's, the revivalists and the reformers to arise?

The reason why you have read this book thus far is because God has enlisted you as a member in the end time army of restoration and reformation. You cannot afford to fail. God is counting on you. It all begins with the passion God has placed within you. Nehemiah was heartbroken about the walls and gates of Jerusalem.

What is it that saddens your heart? What is it that troubles you anytime you see or hear about it? Is it in the Church of today or the media? Maybe anytime you hear the news or watch something on TV? Or is it the children and youth on the streets who perpetuate gun violence? Find out what your passion is... what would you change if you had the opportunity to do so?

God is about to use you as a change agent. Opportunities, access and doors are about to open to you in Jesus Name. I call forth the revival fire to burn from within you in Jesus Name. Receive it now in Jesus Name.

CHAPTER TWO

RESTORATION BEGINS AT THE GATE

Then I said to them, "You see the distress that we are in, how Jerusalem lies waste, and its gates are burned with fire. **Come and let us build the wall of Jerusalem, that we may no longer be a reproach."** *And I told them of the hand of my God which had been good upon me, and also of the king's words that he had spoken to me. So they said,* **"Let us rise up and build." Then they set their hands to this good work.** Neh. 2:17-18

The restoration of Jerusalem began with Nehemiah's leadership in the rebuilding of the burnt gates. Ten gates were rebuilt in order for the city to experience revival. These gates definitely had spiritual significance to restore hope and a future to the children of Israel. The Kingdom of Darkness was uprooted by taking over the gates again. What were these gates and their spiritual significance?

1. Sheep Gate: *"Then Eliashib the high priest rose up with his brethren the priests and built the Sheep Gate; they consecrated it and hung its doors."* Neh. 3:1

The Sheep Gate was the first gate to be mentioned. In the Old Testament the High Priest took the lamb and sheep through this gate into the Temple to be slaughtered for the atonement of sin. We know in the New Testament that Jesus is the sacrificial lamb that was slaughtered for our sins to bring redemption: *"He has appeared to put away sin by the sacrifice of Himself."* Heb. 9:26b

The significance of the sheep gate mentioned first is very strategic. If there will be revival and reformation, we must come in through the Blood of Jesus. Not only did Nehemiah rebuild the sheep gate but also the door connected to the gate. Jesus Christ is the doorway to redemption, the door to the Father, the door to eternal life. So the foundation must be set right. There is power in the Blood of Jesus. The blood symbolizes covenant, it grants us access to the very presence of God and it unleashes the Kingdom of Heaven on earth. When God delivered the children of Israel from the bondage of Egypt He gave Moses instructions for every family of Israel:

*Speak to all the congregation of Israel, saying: 'On the tenth of this month **every man shall take for himself a lamb**, according to the house of his father, a lamb for a household. And if the household is too small for the lamb, let him and his neighbor next to his house take it according to the number of the persons; according to each man's need you shall make your count for the lamb. Your lamb shall be without blemish, a male of the first year. You may take it from the sheep or from the goats. Now you shall keep it until the fourteenth day of the same month. Then the whole assembly of the congregation of Israel shall kill it at twilight. And **they shall take some of the blood and put it on the two doorposts and on the lintel of the houses** where they eat it.* Ex. 12:3-7

Why the lamb and the blood? **Blood is the highest currency in the realm of the spirit.** If you want to see Satan and his demons act up give them blood. There is a reason why people do blood and animal sacrifices. Just as we spend money on physical things in the natural, likewise, the currency in the spirit realm is blood. When you read about God talking about blood in scripture, there is a transaction that is being made. Now it will make sense to us why I Cor. 6:20a say: *"For you were **bought** at a price"*. The Greek word used for *'bought'* is *'agorazo'* which means 'to go to market', 'to purchase', 'to redeem'.

> *Blood is the highest currency in the realm of the spirit.*

There is no deliverance outside the Blood of Jesus. All throughout Scripture, you never see any revival or redemption without the shedding of blood. That is the foundation. The Power in the Blood of Jesus is stronger than any satanic covenant, powers of darkness holding people, cities, and nations in captivity. We need to apply the Blood of Jesus more over Regions, over Families, over the Government, the Senate and over businesses, etc. As we apply the Blood, we release the Power therein to dislodge and dismantle the powers of darkness which are in operation. We need to decree souls saved by releasing the Blood of Jesus for their salvation.

Not only was Jesus the sacrificial lamb for redemption, He also modeled the life of a leader for all to follow. If we will see transformation we need to become the sacrificial lamb ourselves. *Too many people talk the talk but don't walk the walk.* To see regional or city transformation it's beyond talking, people must be ready to pay the price. Who is willing to risk their lives for a change?

The freedom we enjoy today in America didn't come cheap. The founding fathers sacrificed their lives for what we are enjoying today. The future of the next generation is in our hands. It is time to take action.

Nehemiah began the revival in his generation by restoring the initial gate: The Sheep Gate. Let's go back to the Blood of Jesus and emphasize on the Power therein against satanic powers. I plead the Blood of Jesus over your life and decree victory right now in every areas of your life in Jesus Name.

2. The Fish Gate: *"Also the sons of Hassenaah built the Fish Gate; they laid its beams and hung its doors with its bolts and bars."* Neh. 3:3

In the Old Testament the fishermen brought fishes through the fish gate to Jerusalem to be sold. This is very symbolic. After the Blood of Jesus has been shed the gospel of the Kingdom must be preached. People must receive Jesus as their Lord and Savior. We need to preach Jesus as the only way to salvation from street to street in

America and even all the way to the Oval Office in the White House. We need to pull down every false religion, false ideologies, man-made philosophies and anti-Christ agendas that has taken over the nation promoting all inclusive religion. Souls need to be won in every sector of the society. If we can get more Senators saved do you know how easy it will be to disapprove and annul many of these satanic agendas infiltrating the society? This is why the Body of Christ needs to lift up their voices in prayers for those in the field of battle in the workforce. However, we must also realize that the salvation gospel is only an entrance to the Kingdom of God. We have to preach the Kingdom Gospel in order to see the totality of God at work. Understanding the Kingdom Gospel will help many minister in the marketplace where it is forbidden to preach the gospel of salvation. We can still preach Christ in several ways and let the Holy Spirit do the work.

Dr. Lance Wallnau has done a very good job in teaching the Body of Christ on some pertinent subjects in his book, "The 7 Mountain Mandate". He teaches how to take the 7 kingdoms of our society for God? This is truly the Kingdom Gospel. I believe this is where the Church at large needs to be sharpened. We have been so narrow minded for centuries, and this last day revival is going to shake the nations not just the churches but the stratums of societies. We must be good fishermen. The harvest is ripe. God is raising a strategic end time army. You must know which division you fall into. All must not preach from the pulpit, some have to go to Hollywood yet their ministries must be accepted and respected like we do the world evangelist who does mega crusades. We must start embracing what Apostle Paul taught about in 1 Corinthians 12:5-6 *"There are differences of ministries, but the same Lord. And there are diversities of activities, but it is the same God who works all in all. [7] But the manifestation of the Spirit is given to each one for the profit of all"*.

> *Every career must be seen as a ministry.*

The fullness of God is not being seen in our generation. The revival fire is not burning as expected because of myopic mindset of the Church. We have limited God for too long. There are some who are already catching up to this move of God already, but we need more Christians to grow into maturity. *Every career must be seen as a ministry.*

Fishing was a lucrative career in the Old Testament days as well as the days of Jesus. Yet, Jesus used it as a symbolic term for soul winning and the Kingdom Gospel: *"Then He said to them, "Follow Me, and I will make you fishers of men."* Matthew 4:19. Pray right now and receive your hook to start fishing for the Lord in the Name of Jesus. Father let everyone reading this book become a fisher of souls for you in Jesus Name. I pray that our churches will begin to birth Kingdom ministries in the Name of Jesus; that we will no longer limit you to our four-wall churches anymore.

3. The Old Gate: *"Moreover Jehoiada the son of Paseah and Meshullam the son of Besodeiah repaired the Old Gate; they laid its beams and hung its doors, with its bolts and bars."* Neh. 3:6

This gate in Jerusalem was a very old one. It led to the newer section of the city. Most of the older Jews knew this gate but the newer generation did not. In fact, Christian tradition suggests that Jesus was crucified in close proximity to this gate.

This gate is very symbolic since it connected the old to the new. It means, although the gospel of Jesus or Christianity is considered an old religion, it is applicable to every generation. The story of the Christian Faith might be old but the power thereof is still as fresh as ever.

For every new generation to be transformed we must go back to the old rugged cross of Jesus Christ with applicable methods for today's generation. What I am speaking about connects us to understanding the Kingdom Gospel we addressed prior to this. It is once more, another area I believe which requires more work to be done in the Body of Christ.

This is where the New Age Movement has succeeded in stealing souls from the Church. We have emphasized so much on the judgmental gospel and left out the mercy and grace part and in so doing have lost many to the kingdom of darkness. A lack of understanding the totality of what salvation truly means is the foundational error of many Christians. I wrote extensively in understanding the Christian Faith in my first book: *"Journey of Faith."* There is a balance to everything. Going back to the Old is one thing but the right application to the New is another. If the Old Gate wasn't important, Nehemiah wouldn't waste his time on that project. But he also knew the connection it would make to the coming revival in his days.

We need to learn the principles of the Bible and understand them as they relate to today. This is practical faith; kingdom living. It will not only help us experience heaven on earth but also unleash heaven in others as well. A typical example will be the principle of diligence: *"Seest thou a man diligent in his business? He shall stand before kings; he shall not stand before mean men."* Proverbs 22:29

> **Revelation will help us to overcome the Devil.**

This is an old scripture King Solomon wrote in his days but it is still applicable today for anyone that wants to succeed in any career, adventure, or workplace. *Diligence is not an option to get to the pinnacle of success but a must.* While we are praying and binding occult powers in the High Place we must also learn to be diligent in our work as well. The promise is that such a person will be lifted or promoted to the High Place. Prayer without diligence will not do this. So the old time religionist might tell people to focus solely on prayer - after all Jesus started by prayer and ended by prayer. That is not the total truth. Jesus' ministry started by Him understanding the prophecies concerning Him in the Old Testament and He applied them in His day by submitting Himself to John the Baptist for baptism. (Matt. 4:15). *Understanding will help us to pray the right kinds of prayers. Revelation will help us to overcome the Devil.* It is revelation by the Spirit that teaches us how to apply the principles of God's Word.

The World is in chaos and many are looking for solutions. The occult kingdoms are busy fixing satanic agendas to meet the needs of the people while the Church is busy criticizing one another. Let's go back to how the Prophets of old did it in their time. Let's find out what made them succeed. Nehemiah travelled back into time before he went forward with the mission of rebuilding the walls of Jerusalem:

> ***Remember, I pray, the word that You commanded Your servant Moses,*** *saying, 'If you are unfaithful, I will scatter you among the nations; but if you return to Me, and keep My commandments and do them, though some of you were cast out to the farthest part of the heavens, yet I will gather them from there, and bring them to the place which I have chosen as a dwelling for My name.' Now these are Your servants and Your people, whom You have redeemed by Your great power, and by Your strong*

*hand. O Lord, I pray, please let Your ear be attentive to the prayer of Your servant, and to the prayer of Your servants who desire to fear Your name; and let **Your servant prosper this day**, I pray, and grant him mercy in the sight of this man.* Neh. 1:8-11

Everything under heaven has its root in the spirit realm. One of the gateways to the Spirit realm is the Word of God. The Bible is full of principles. The principles are the laws of the Kingdom.

There is nothing hidden under the sun, history is only repeating itself in a different format. You can find almost all professions which exist today in the Bible but in different terminology and different ways of operation. A Governor or President can learn how to govern a city or nation merely by understanding the Book of Deuteronomy. It is time to go back to the principles of the Bible if we will transform today's generation.

Please pray right now that the Lord will anoint you with wisdom and revelation knowledge of Him in His Word that will help you conquer and occupy territories for Him in Jesus Name. Pray now that just like He revealed the mysteries of the Kingdom to the Apostles and Prophets of

Old, He should do the same for you in Jesus Name. I release the oil of wisdom and revelation upon you right now in the Name of Jesus. Begin to possess territories for God in Jesus Name.

4. The Valley Gate: *"Hanun and the inhabitants of Zanoah repaired the Valley Gate. They built it, hung its doors with its bolts and bars, and repaired a thousand cubits of the wall as far as the Refuse Gate."*
Neh. 3:13

Jerusalem had several valleys around the hill top where tombs were located. The hilltop was for stars, greatness, and influential people. Probably that was why Jesus likened the Christian to a city set on a hill: *"Ye are the light of the world. A city that is set on an hill cannot be hid"* Matt. 5:14

The children of Israel were a special people chosen by God through whom He was to reveal Himself to the other nations. They were to be the light that would lead other nations in the right path, (Is. 2:2) but in Nehemiah's day, they were in the tomb. Their gates were burnt down and their walls were broken. They were buried. Today, the Church ought to be the light of the world - Christians ought to be the city set on the hill. Where are we today? Are we on the mountain or in the tomb?

You see why Nehemiah had to rebuild the valley gate? It symbolized resurrection from every spiritual death. Where is the Power in the Church? Where is the fire of revival in our cities? Where is God in our nations? We need to wake up. Great destinies have been put to sleep. It is time for restoration. We need to resurrect our prayer lives, our study lives, our fellowship lives, our evangelistic lives, our Pentecostal lives and above all our lives that reveal God.

Please join me in prayer right now and command every spiritual, evil tomb housing your destiny, potential and skills to be destroyed right now in Jesus Name. I command my glory to arise in Jesus Name. We cast out the spiritual death out of our churches, out of our marriages, out of our schools, out of our businesses. I decree revival in every life reading this book in Jesus Name.

Every demonic tomb that has swallowed the businesses in our cities, we decree be broken and declare restoration of businesses in Jesus Name.

5. The Refuse Gate: *"Malchijah the son of Rechab Leader of the district of Beth Haccerem, repaired the Refuse Gate; he built it and hung its doors with its bolts and bars."* Neh. 3:14

I concur with Rhoel Lomahan in his exposition of the Dung Gate of Nehemiah: *"The Dung Gate was where people brought out their garbage. A healthy city needs a place to take out the trash. The Dung Gate was probably the least appealing place to work, but we can notice in verse 14 that the person who worked there was a ruler."*[5]

You will notice that the Refuse Gate is connected to the previous Valley Gate. There is a symbolic meaning here I would like to share with you. The tomb is connected to the dump. As the people brought their trash and dump it at the Refuse Gate; they were saying good bye to something that was no longer useful to them.

The Church ought to be the light and the city on the hill but when the church is in the tomb it experiences spiritual death. And people's problems and issues are the trashes. They come and dump their worries and concerns in the church, yet the church has not been able to offer them solutions. It seems as though people come with problems and leave with more problems. Where is the Church of Jesus Christ? It makes so much sense why Jesus said:

> *And Levi made him a great feast in his own house: and there was a great company of publicans and of others that sat down with them. But their scribes and Pharisees murmured against his disciples, saying, Why do ye eat and drink with publicans and sinners? And Jesus answering said unto them, **They that are whole need not a physician; but they that are sick.** I came not to call the righteous, but sinners to repentance.* Luke 5:29-32

The world is full of sick people. The painful part is that the church as well is full of sick people, yet there are hardly any healings taking place in our congregations. People are sick in their bodies, in their minds, in their finances, in their marriages, in their families. The cities are sick. Lord we need revival. Send your fire again like the day of Pentecost in the Name of Jesus.

The world is looking for transformational leaders that will undertake the task that other people will naturally run from. That was exactly what *Malchijah,* the Leader who rebuilt the refuse gate did. He laid aside his pride. He was a humble man who had Kingdom vision. We need visionaries who will see beyond the pulpit and take the gospel of Jesus to the dying world.

The reason why there are so many churches in the tomb is because they left the Great Commission and focused on the Great Collection. And the reason why there are so many frustrated Christians in the world today is because they left the witnessing assignment for their Pastors and focused on greener pastures.

Please don't misunderstand me. I am not against money. Money is a tool. I cannot preach the gospel across the globe if I don't have some kind of financial support.

I thank God for all the pillars and supporters of our ministries. But if I focus on how much money I make rather than the impact I make, then I have left preaching the gospel of Jesus Christ. I am no longer serving God but Mammon.

You don't put the cart before the horse. True prosperity comes from God. God wants us to be wealthy, (Deut. 8:18,) but He also wants us to be obedient, (Is. 1:18). The problem Christians have is that they allow their issues to overwhelm them and in so doing, they find it difficult not only to obey God but also to believe Him. Please read this scripture slowly: *"But without faith it is impossible to please him: for he that cometh to God must believe that he is, and that he is a rewarder of them that diligently seek him."* Hebrews 11:6

God rewards obedience and faithfulness. Every Christian ought to be a leader because we are the Light of the World. When you are a light you lead people out of darkness. However, what we are experiencing today is that more Christians are being led into darkness rather than conquering the darkness.

Transformational Leadership comes with sacrifice for others. You must be willing to pay the price for the blessing you seek.

At one point in my life and ministry my wife and I had only one vehicle and my busy schedule, (especially with my church duties) always warranted me to need the car. Constantly, I had to sacrifice my personal business in order to meet the needs of the ministry and my family. It was very strenuous, but we kept believing God for a new car. Eventually, God answered our prayers by asking me to go plant a new church in another city. Anyway, we tried everything we could to raise enough money for the new project and still did not meet our goal. By faith we travelled and had an awesome crusade which enabled us to plant a new church. God supplied all our needs with overflow. By the time we returned, I heard God said to me: 'Now you can go pick up your new car". I was dumbfounded. I obeyed God by going to look for a used vehicle I thought I could afford but God had His own plan. He gave me a brand new vehicle that came right out of the factory. It was a miracle and I bless the Name of the Lord. I needed something physical, God needed His harvest of souls. I put God first and He blessed me beyond my wildest dream.

It's the same principle with Abraham in Genesis 22. God will always test you. Where is your heart? Are you ready to do what others wouldn't do for God and watch Him use you as a change agent in this generation? Who knows, maybe that is why God has you reading this page right now? Please pray and ask God for Grace to obey Him all the way in Jesus Name.

Lord, let your grace be released right now to the life of your child in Jesus Name. I decree the unction to do exploit come upon you. Receive the grace for service.

6. The Fountain Gate: *"Shallun the son of Col-Hozeh, leader of the district of Mizpah, repaired the Fountain Gate; he built it, covered it, hung its doors with its bolts and bars, and repaired the wall of the Pool of Shelah by the King's Garden, as far as the stairs that go down from the City of David."* Neh. 3:15

The Fountain Gate is another symbolic gate. It led to the Pool of Siloam in the Temple. It was this same pool that Jesus healed a blind man:

> *When he had thus spoken, he spat on the ground, and made clay of the spittle, and he anointed the eyes of the blind man with the clay, And said unto him, Go, wash in the pool of Siloam, (which is by interpretation, Sent.) He went his way therefore, and washed, and came seeing.* John 9:6-7

The Fountain Gate represents the Spirit of God. This is the Holy Spirit that confirms God's word with signs and wonders. It is this Spirit that manifest miracles. It makes the difference. Jesus was the Word made flesh. He spoke to the blind man to go to Siloam after applying the clay on his eyes. The blind man heard 'the Word,' (Jesus) and Jesus spoke 'Rhema' to him. The blind man came back seeing because the Spirit of God confirmed the Word of Jesus with miracles. The only word that produces miracles

58

is the word that proceeds from the mouth of God which is the Rhema word; (spoken word). The reason why we don't see miracles today as we ought to is because we have too many Christians who are spiritually deaf and blind. The Holy Spirit is the fountain gate that unleashes miracles. The Power is behind that gate but only the Holy Spirit can grant access to that power. The gate code you need to gain access to power is *'the Voice of God'*; *'the Word from God'*. There are many who are spiritually blind and deaf, now you wonder why we have so many depressed people in the world.

That man in the above Scripture became a beggar not by choice but by his health condition. Too many people are in the wrong career and are so depressed. They hate what they do. Some take anti-depressant just to keep them going. There is a solution. The Devil has them in bondage. Today we possess that gate of your mind in the Name of Jesus.

There is nothing like the ability to hear and see things in the Spirit. If you can hear God and see where He is taking you that will be the end of your misery. Nobody is a victim of chance. You were purposefully made by God. But only your maker can give you the blue print of your destiny. That was why David said:

"Open thou mine eyes, that I may behold wondrous things out of thy law." Psalm 119:19

"Thy word is a lamp unto my feet, and a light unto my path." Psalm 119:105

How victorious your life will be if you can hear from God and see every step of the way where God is taking you? Do you know that you can defeat the Devil when you hear God? The Word He speaks to you becomes a sword in your hand. So anytime the Devil comes against you, (which he will always do,) you can defeat him only with the sword not with your tears, complaint or murmuring. The one person the Devil respects is the one with a sword who knows how to use it. Ask Jesus in Matt. 4:4.

At one time when I was newly born again, I kept having severe attacks from the marine kingdom. I was experiencing sexual intercourse in my dreams which led to my being raped in my dreams. Many times I woke up so weak, soaked with sweat but most of all, frustrated. The enemy was stealing my glory and I didn't know what to do. I prayed so hard using every pertinent scripture I could think about in the Word of God. It seemed like the more I prayed the more severe the attacks occurred. Satan was having a fun ride with me. I ran to my pastors who prayed and prayed for me including pouring oil on my head yet it wouldn't stop. At one time I stopped telling people about it because I was so ashamed and I felt like God was refusing to deliver me. Until one day while I was praying, I heard a voice within me said to me: "why don't you ask me to teach you how to pray?" That is exactly what Scripture teaches: *"Likewise the Spirit also helpeth our infirmities: for we know not what we should pray for as we ought: but the Spirit itself maketh intercession for us with groanings which cannot be uttered."* Romans 8:26

So I changed my pattern of prayer and asked the Holy Spirit to help me. It all started by me hearing the Rhema word, then I heard Him say to me to study 1 Cor. 6:20. This was the beginning of my deliverance from marine attacks. I studied that Scripture and saw something different. It dawned on me (in a new way) that God actually bought me; He redeemed me and purchased me with a price. He paid for my deliverance. I got upset in the Spirit. It was a Holy anger. I fought the Devil, daring him to come near me next time. I was so confident and happy that I belonged to God. I broke every hold the Devil had on me using the Rhema word that had been illuminated in my Spirit. That night I had another dream. This time the demon came to oppress me as usual but it was different. I had a sword in my hand and I dipped the sword in a burning furnace. It was red hot at the tip of the sword. When the demon saw it, it fled and never came back. I got my deliverance, thanks to Jesus.

The sword, the spoken word and the burning fire was the revealed word. When you use both, I dare the Devil to stand in your way. Every Christian is entitled to this covenant right. You can have it right where you are.

Like Nehemiah, you have to repossess that fountain gate of your life that has burned down or hijacked by the Devil. A fountain springs water. Your heart, your belly, your Spirit being is your fountain.

> *"In the last day, that great day of the feast, Jesus stood and cried, saying, If any man thirst, let him come unto me, and drink. He that believeth on me, as the scripture hath said, out of his belly shall flow rivers of living water."* John 7:37-38

This Holy Spirit was the key to Jesus' success in ministry. He came down on the day of Pentecost (Acts 2) and has remained on earth since then. He is the source of every revival. He is constantly looking for those who desire him. He transforms and empowers as well. The key to receiving this Power, this flow from the Spirit, is thirst. How thirsty are you? How bad do you want it? When you have the current flowing through you, it is possible to pray for hours. Your spiritual eyes and spiritual ears will be opened. You will flow in Power that destroys the powers of darkness. You will reign in life. This is the secret to a successful and victorious Christian life. Do you want this Power? Would you ask the Lord Jesus right now to open the fountain deep in the inside of you? Ask the Lord Jesus to baptize you in the Power of the Holy Ghost. Tell Him you want to flow in power from today. Command your spiritual ears to open to hear the Rhema word from heaven in Jesus Name.

Now, I stand in the gap for you and declare the Heavens open on you right now. Let the Power of the Holy Spirit rest upon you for signs and wonders in Jesus Name.

7. The Water Gate: *"Moreover the Nethinim who dwelt in Ophel made repairs as far as the place in front of the Water Gate toward the east, and on the projecting tower."* Neh. 3:26

This is another symbolic gate. The Water gate was next to the Fountain gate. Since the Fountain gate represents the Spirit of God, the Water gate represents the Word of God. The Spirit and the Word must go hand in hand in order to see the power of God manifested with signs of personal transformation and revival.

> *So Ezra the priest brought the Law before the assembly of men and women and all who could hear with understanding on the first day of the seventh month. Then he read from it in the open square that was in front of the Water Gate from morning until midday, before the men and women and those who could understand; and the ears of all the people were attentive to the Book of the Law.* Neh. 8:2-3

Like I emphasized in the Fountain gate exposition, the Word *from* God is the gate code or access code to power. The fountain gate is the transformer that produces the electrons; the current that supplies power. It must be tuned by the Rhema Word of God. This is how to defeat the Devil. The Word must move from the written to the spoken Word. The Voice of God is what the Devil cannot stand; it destabilizes the kingdom of darkness and shatters powers of darkness. The Voice of God has so much power.

The voice of the LORD is over the waters; The God of glory thunders; The LORD is over many waters. The voice of the LORD is powerful; The voice of the LORD is full of majesty. The voice of the LORD breaks the cedars, Yes, the LORD splinters the cedars of Lebanon. He makes them also skip like a calf, Lebanon and Sirion like a young wild ox. The voice of the LORD divides the flames of fire. The voice of the LORD shakes the wilderness; The LORD shakes the Wilderness of Kadesh. Psalm 29:3-8

The Voice of God is the trigger of Power. When the voice of God comes upon the written Word then the Word becomes activated; ready to be unleashed. This Rhema word is the Sword of the Spirit you need for battle at any time. Receive the Word from the Lord today in Jesus Name.

8.   The Horse Gate: *"Beyond the Horse Gate the priests made repairs, each in front of his own house."* Neh. 3:28

The Horse Gate is a very strategic gate. The Horse Gate was located next to the horse stables where the people prepared for warfare. Horses were used in war. So when the

Bible mentions horses what comes to mind is spiritual warfare which is what this book is essentially about.

Nehemiah knew if they would rebuild the city then they had to be ready also for some warfare. It is amazing how the rebuilding of the gates was sequential as you can see. It was not coincidental at all. It was done strategically. The horse gate immediately followed the water and fountain gates. When you have the Spirit of God, the Word of God now you are ready to possess. The reason for warfare is simply to declare who is in charge of a territory.

The Body of Christ needs to rebuild this horse gate again if we will see revival. We need to start teaching our people the art of spiritual warfare if we want believers to live a victorious Christian life.

In this chapter, I would like to support this writing with some real life experiences and testimonies of people who had fought the Devil strategically and won so that your faith can be boosted.

We had recent testimonies in one of our branch church that moved the congregants to tears. As I sat down I looked at the congregation praising the Name of the Lord as they heard the victories God granted these families. We saw the Lordship of Jesus; the Kingdom of God manifesting in the lives of His people and in our Church family.

A brother shared his testimony of how he had been unemployed for eight years. Now, this man is a college graduate and a family man with children. Can you imagine the kind of frustration he went through for so many years, unable to get a job? This happened to him because he was oppressed by the Devil. He had been to so many unsuccessful interviews until he joined our church and he learnt the art of spiritual warfare through strategic prayers and fasting. He learnt his rights in Christ Jesus and how the Devil had stolen his joy.

After several intense prayer sessions he finally got a job. Eight years of joblessness was broken. However, the Devil didn't stop fighting because within one month he lost the job that he was so glad to obtain. When he told me that he lost his job, I told him that was not God. Satan had stolen his testimony and his job and we had to get it back.

During this same time period, God instructed me prophetically to wash the feet of our members for possession of things that belong to them. After his feet washing, he was spiritually prepared to obtain his possessions so the next day he went back to the office that previously got rid of him. He took all the required documents, praying and trusting that the position was still open. Please understand that he lives in a metropolitan region where jobs are hard to find. God in His infinite mercy kept this position waiting for him. No one occupied his seat until he came back to the job. He was asked to resume his position effective immediately, no questions asked. That is the God we serve. We exercised our faith and bruised the head of the Devil who tried to frustrate God's son.

Please allow me to convey another testimony of a member of our church. This woman happened to be a well respected, highly regarded career woman in the society. The Devil stole her joy for years by taking her oldest daughter away from her along with her grand kids. The Devil tried to put enmity between her and her daughter for years. She wanted her daughter to come home someday. On a faithful day I was led to do some spiritual warfare prayers in her house; anointing every corner of that house and destroying every demonic stronghold by the power of Holy Ghost. The Lord gave me a prophetic word for her that stated that by Christmas she will be enjoying a family restoration and a family reunion. In my spirit I was certain that her daughter would be home with the grand kids and they all will be eating and dining as a family. I would like to declare that it came to pass according to the word of the Lord.

All of this happened after the feet washing and spiritual warfare. This family was able to testify to the goodness of our God. If that was not enough that Sunday morning, we had another woman testify that her daughter left for five months returned home and was present at church that morning. We had both families testify. This is the goodness of God. Victory over the Devil indeed was what we were celebrating that Sunday morning.

This is what every believer ought to enjoy every day of their lives. Miracles should be an everyday occurrence in a Christian's life. But for some reason the Devil has many bound. That is why this book is important. You are reading this because God wants to liberate you and also use you to liberate others. Was this not what Jesus meant? *"So ought not this woman, being a daughter of Abraham, whom Satan has bound—think of it—for eighteen years, be loosed from this bond on the Sabbath?"* Luke 13:16. This is what the world needs to see happening in the Body of Christ if our gospel will every make an impact in the society. There are too many people bound by the Devil, we need to set them free. It won't come easy. First, we have to bind the strongman because that is where the spiritual warfare is.

According to our key text, each Priest built this gate in front of their own houses. That was very strategic because the Priests were essentially taking charge of their homes. Nothing went in or out without first going through them. They drew the line and were ready for warfare. The Horse Gate, remember, is solely for war.

Every believer is a King and Priest: *"And hast made us unto our God kings and priests: and we shall reign on the earth."* Rev. 5:10. Kings are warriors, Priests are worshippers. Your body is the house of God. So as you present your body as a living sacrifice in worshipping God you also protect your life from satanic attack and possession through spiritual warfare. That was what the Priest did in Nehemiah's days. Each home, each family, each believer ought to put the Devil where he belongs which is under your feet. Each one ought to know how to fight spiritual warfare strategically.

9. **The East Gate:** *"After them repaired Zadok the son of Immer over against his house. After him repaired also Shemaiah the son of Shechaniah, the keeper of the east gate."* Neh. 3:29

This was the gate that Jesus will come through when He returns.

> *And his feet shall stand in that day upon the mount of Olives, which is before Jerusalem on the east, and the mount of Olives shall cleave in the midst thereof toward the east and toward the west, and there shall be a very great valley; and half of the mountain shall remove toward the north, and half of it toward the south.* Zech.14:4

This gate represents the gospel of consummation of the age; the return of Christ. As we live we are to prepare the way for Jesus' return. He is coming back and He is coming soon. We must be watchful and be alert.

10. The Gate Miphkad: *"After him repaired Malchiah the goldsmith's son unto the place of the Nethinims, and of the merchants, over against the gate Miphkad, and to the going up of the corner."* Neh. 3:31

This was the last gate built in the restoration project. As I explained previously, there is no coincidence in all of these gates. There is a reason why it was

71

sequentially arranged. The Miphkad gate followed the East gate which symbolically means the return of Jesus. Now while we await His return this Miphkad gate must be built and possessed. To understand this is to pay attention to the two Hebrew words used in the above text: *'Malchiah'* which means *'King'* and *'Miphkad'* which means *'Assignment'*.

Hitherto, it symbolically means that Jesus although is coming back not as a suffering Messiah but as the King of Kings. Before He comes He has appointed and commissioned us to reign, subdue the earth and get it ready for His arrival. He has made us Kings, (Rev. 5:10). Kings conquer territories. That was why He said we should: *'occupy till He comes'* (Luke 19:13). Do you know what it means to occupy? It means to possess territories. It means to claim ownership. We have been appointed by the King of Kings to claim ownership over the earth till He comes. When He comes, He will be riding on a white Horse ready for judgment and war:

> *And I saw heaven opened, and **behold a white horse**; and he that sat upon him was called Faithful and True, and in righteousness he doth judge and make war. His eyes were as a flame of fire, and on*

*his head were many crowns; and he had a name written, that no man knew, but he himself. And he was clothed with a vesture dipped in blood: and **his name is called The Word of God. And the armies which were in heaven followed him upon white horses**,* clothed in fine linen, white and clean. ***And out of his mouth goeth a sharp sword, that with it he should smite the nations:*** *and he shall rule them with a rod of iron: and he treadeth the winepress of the fierceness and wrath of Almighty God. And he hath on his vesture and on his thigh a name written,* ***KING OF KINGS, AND LORD OF LORDS.*** Rev. 19:11-16

CHAPTER THREE

WATCHMEN ON THE WALL

"The Church," needs to be in position of unity and agreement in prayer.

We have learnt so much about the restoration and the rebuilding of gates as a strategic tool for spiritual warfare. We must take charge of the gates so that we can successfully gain control of the land. That is one aspect. Now, you cannot possess the gates by ignoring the walls. There cannot be gates if there are no walls. Remember the key scripture we started with in part 2 of the book, (Nehemiah 1:3b). This scripture states that not only were the gates burnt but the walls were broken down also. This is also very significant. Walls are made up of bricks joined together into a formidable unit. *This means unity... agreement in prayer.* If the gate entrances to our society, land, cities, nations, families will be protected, then the spiritual guards, *"The Church,"* need to be in position of unity and agreement in prayer. I am not talking about just

74

ordinary prayer but intercessory, prophetic and warfare prayer to make sure that the walls and gates don't fall down.

This was exactly what happened in Nehemiah's days. The Devil is always busy. He didn't want peace to reign. He did not want to lose a territory he once possessed. He would do anything to repossess it again including possessing those that are least expected to be agents of Satan.

> But it so happened, when Sanballat heard **that we were rebuilding the wall, that he was furious and very indignant,** and mocked the Jews. And he spoke before his brethren and the army of Samaria, and said, "What are these feeble Jews doing? Will they fortify themselves? Will they offer sacrifices? Will they complete it in a day? Will they revive the stones from the heaps of rubbish—stones that are burned?"Now Tobiah the Ammonite was beside him, and he said, "Whatever they build, if even a fox goes up on it, he will break down their stone wall." Hear, O our God, for we are despised; turn their reproach on their own heads, and give them as plunder to a land of captivity! Do not cover their

*iniquity, and do not let their sin be blotted out from before You; for they have provoked You to anger before the builders. So we built the wall, and the entire wall was joined together up to half its height, for the people had a mind to work. Now it happened, when Sanballat, Tobiah, the Arabs, the Ammonites, and the Ashdodites heard **that the walls of Jerusalem were being restored and the gaps were beginning to be closed, that they became very angry,** and **all of them conspired together to come and attack Jerusalem and create confusion.** Nevertheless we made our prayer to our God, and **because of them we set a watch against them day and night.*** Neh. 4:1-9

Please pay close attention to the highlighted verses in the above scripture to better understand my exposition in this chapter.

Common sense should tell anyone at that time in Jerusalem that Nehemiah and his team meant well for Jerusalem. The city and the people were totally in disarray, captivity and shame. Here were a people whom God had chosen to be an example of His greatness in that region but they were experiencing nothing but opposition from the enemy. The Devil knew he was losing his ground so what he did was raise up agents from their own people against the restoration project. The bible says in Nehemiah that Sanballat's Jewish allies kept Sanballat and Tobiah informed concerning the progress of the work.

There is nothing as painful as seeing your own brothers and sisters opposing you when they should be the ones building with you. Nehemiah must have felt so much the pain as a result of this betrayal.

What Nehemiah experienced is exactly what is going on in the Body of Christ… rather than building and expanding God's kingdom *we are busy tearing each other down* out of jealousy, envy, and bitterness; born out of competition. The Devil has succeeded in sowing the seed of competition in the hearts of many. When this seed is planted, they lose sight of whose team they are on and they are mainly concerned with doing things bigger or better than their brethren. Who gets the glory? The fivefold ministry ought to complete one another not compete with one another. No one has it all; *we see in part and prophesy in part.* Until we grow to maturity in this area it might be difficult to occupy and conquer territories as we ought to. That is the reason why there still is constant warfare on the gates of the cities and nations. By now we should be in charge. This is as a result of the walls not being joined together.

You will notice that the highlighted verse in the above scripture: Neh. 4:7 says '*when Sanballat, Tobiah, the Arabs, the Ammonites, and the Ashdodites*' heard that the *gaps were being closed* in the walls then they became very angry. They were not just angry but very angry. Why? The gaps were being closed; at this point it was going to be hard for the enemy to see what was going on behind the walls and gates. There were no more loop holes. That is what the kingdom of darkness hate. The Devil cannot penetrate if there are no open doors or loop holes. We need to close the gaps and seal the holes in our churches, in our finances, in our families and in our spiritual lives so the Devil doesn't gain his ground anymore. How do we close up the gaps? It is through the prayer of intercession, the prayer of warfare, and prophetic prayers born of the spirit.

What did the Devil do against Nehemiah - he stirred up confusion against them. Wherever there is unity and agreement there is bound to be progress, (Gen. 11). The Devil is the source of confusion. He stirs up confusion so that he can hinder the anointing on the lives of God's children from blessing and restoring the lost. He is a big time loser. *"Again I say to you that if two of you agree on earth concerning anything that they ask, it will be done for them by My Father in heaven."* Matt. 18:19. Would you agree with me right now and pray?

We come in the Name of Jesus and bind every demonic force holding the Body of Christ, cities, nations and regions in captivity. We decree deliverance by the Blood of Jesus and the Power of Holy Ghost. We cast out the spirit of confusion and release the spirit of peace and unity in our homes, churches and cities in the name of Jesus. We close every gap, we seal every spiritual hole and we silence every demonic voice. We decree the Kingdom of God come and reign in this country now and forever more. Amen.

PART THREE

PULLING DOWN ANCIENT GATES

INTRODUCTION

Lift up your heads, O you gates! And be lifted up, you everlasting doors! And the King of glory shall come in. Who is this King of glory? The LORD strong and mighty, The LORD mighty in battle. Lift up your heads, O you gates! Lift up, you everlasting doors! And the King of glory shall come in. Who is this King of glory? The LORD of hosts, He is the King of glory. Psalm 24:7-10

There are ancient powers that have been in existence before the creation of man. Previously, we have learned about Lucifer and his fallen angels who were cast out into the realm of darkness and have been systematically in operation ever since. The kingdom of darkness has been formed into an organized army, so we have to be wise in spiritual warfare to know how to demolish their hierarchical structure if we will possess the gates of the enemy.

This chapter will focus on the leadership heads in the kingdom of darkness. They are the officers in the army of satanic kingdoms. Bypassing the Generals in the army will mean lack of understanding of the tactics of warfare.

When you take out the head you take out the army. *"For we do not wrestle against flesh and blood, but against principalities."* Eph. 6:12a

Principalities are the lead demons in the army. The Bible sometimes refers to them as Princes. They are an assigned company of demons over jurisdictions and regions. They are the commanders in the army. They give orders to other demons. They hold the keys to spiritual gates. So you cannot take over a city or area of influence without subjecting them or overthrowing them. This was what Daniel was taught about when his prayers were hindered as a result of the prince of the Kingdom of Persia.

Then he said to me, "Do not fear, Daniel, for from the first day that you set your heart to understand, and to humble yourself before your God, your words were heard; and I have come because of your words. But the prince of the kingdom of Persia withstood me twenty-one days; and behold, Michael, one of the chief princes, came to help me, for I had been left alone there with the kings of Persia. Dan. 10:12-13

Prophet Daniel's prayer was hindered by a Principality. Which means the Principality of the Air over Persia refused the angel of God entrance through the gate. The Angels of God had to fight their way through. This is serious people of God. The Principality controls what happens in that region, can you believe that. Some might probably say well that was the Old Testament. Again, theological blindness has kept the Body of Christ in bondage for some time. Hear what the Apostle Paul said about Principalities: *"And you He made alive, who were dead in trespasses and sins, in which you once walked according to the course of this world, according to **the prince of the power of the air, the spirit who now works in the sons of disobedience.**"* Eph. 2:1-2

The Scripture never said they no longer exist, it went on to say that it's even at work as we speak; causing people to be disobedient. Was it not Satan who caused Adam and Eve to be disobedient in the Garden of Eden?

These Principalities must be subdued if we will conquer territories... if we will possess any gate as we ought to. So in the subsequent chapters we will focus on some of the key generals in the army of darkness that holds keys of gates in the realm of darkness that must be subdued. It is time we experience changes in our lives, families, cities, nation, and organization. Remember whoever controls the gate control the people.

CHAPTER ONE

THE MARINE KINGDOM

If there is any ancient kingdom that has great influence demonically on people it is the Marine or water spirits. Some of the demons that were cast out of heaven took resident in the water and established themselves there. The Principality of this kingdom is a strong, stubborn and subtle one. They don't give up their prey easily, at least not without a fight.

This was one of the Principalities Moses had to fight in order to conquer Egypt and set the Israelites free.

So the LORD said to Moses: "Pharaoh's heart is hard; he refuses to let the people go. ***Go to Pharaoh in the morning, when he goes out to the water,*** *and you shall stand by the river's bank to meet him; and the rod which was turned to a serpent you shall take in your hand. And you shall say to him, 'The LORD God of the Hebrews has sent me to you, saying, "Let My people go, that they may serve Me in the wilderness"; but indeed, until now you would not hear! Thus says the LORD: "By this you shall know that I am the LORD. Behold, I will* *strike the waters which are in the river with the rod that is in my hand, and they shall be turned to blood. And the fish that are in the river shall die, the river shall stink, and the Egyptians will loathe to drink the water of the river." Then the LORD spoke to Moses, "Say to Aaron,* **'Take your rod and stretch out your hand over the waters of Egypt, over their streams, over their rivers, over their ponds, and over all their pools of water, that they may become blood.** *And there shall be blood throughout all the land of Egypt, both in buckets of wood and pitchers of stone.'" And Moses and Aaron did so, just as the LORD commanded. So he lifted up the rod and struck the waters that were in the river, in the sight of Pharaoh and in the sight of his servants. And all the waters that were in the river were turned to blood. The fish that were in the river died, the river stank, and the Egyptians could not drink the water of the river. So there was blood throughout all the land of Egypt. Ex.7:14-21*

Why the river in Egypt? The Egyptians were idolaters. They worshipped several gods. But one of their strongholds in Egypt was the Marine god and goddess. Egyptians worshipped the river god; a goddess called *Hapy* - god of

87

the Nile; '*Hat-Mehit*'- Fish goddess and Isis – goddess of protection. Now you will understand the reason why God asked Moses to stretch the rod over the Nile River. The River gods and goddesses were the Principalities that empowered Pharaoh. He visited them in the morning. Only God knows what he did when he went there every morning as is highlighted in the above Scripture. Pharaoh would not be that dedicated and committed to going there every morning if there was nothing to offer. It was beyond just starring at the fishes or putting flowers in the stream; that could be done anytime of the day. He certainly was paying homage to that ancient Principality. The more the people drink from that water the more they were entrapped spiritually and physically. Can you imagine that?

The nature of the Marine powers can be easily detected if you know how they operate. Amongst many; their attributes are sexual enticement, spirit husbands and spirit wives, sexual intercourse in dreams, unstable relationships, broken marriages, and singleness for a long time. This is because they are already betrothed to a marine demon knowingly or unknowingly. These demons can be very jealous and will not allow any other man or woman to be in a relationship with them.

Financial difficulties are one of their methods of punishment to those possessed by them. If someone who is under the influence of this spirit disobeys their rules and get married or if they decide to leave their kingdom, they are punished with financial challenges. Another way they punish people is barrenness, this is common with women who had had some dealings with them in their past.

This is not strange to some of us from Africa. It is one of the strongholds for those who came from riverside communities. Some of our forefathers worshipped these gods before the emancipation of Christianity. Most times when covenant are made with this Principalities, it includes the family as a whole not just individuals. That is one reason why many today suffer all kinds of oppression from the Marine kingdom and as much as they pray, they don't see changes or it reoccurs after a short while because the covenant with the Marine Powers is yet to be broken. Blood always symbolizes or seals a covenant deal. Moses had to stretch the rod over the Nile River and cause it to be bloody so that the Children of Israel would receive their deliverance. The Blood of Jesus is stronger today. It can destroy any demonic covenant. The good news is just like Moses we have the rod today. It is time to use it. It must be applied to every marine stronghold contending against you, against your family, finances and city, etc. Any city where you find sexual promiscuity on the rise it's because the Marine Principality is in charge there. Sexual enticement, lust, etc is one of their strongest devices. They also like to hold people's destiny in bondage like they did with the children of Israel. Slavery is one their methods in dealing with people financially.

I prayed for a business man who had a lucrative business which was strategically located in a very busy city. There is no way you could miss his business if you drove past the sign but for some reason he discovered that customers drove past his store to other businesses located at the corner which were not well exposed like his. He was on the verge of closing down the business, until a friend invited him to one of my prophetic meetings. While I was ministering under the Power of the Holy Spirit, I was led to minister deliverance to those under Marine bondage; the Word of Knowledge came for him. I had never met him before. After the meeting he took me to his store. We prayed in front of this store. Suddenly my spiritual eyes were opened and I saw a gate shut against his business by marine spirits. One of his competitors had gone to a marine priest to divert customers from seeing his business. So people were driving past his store without seeing it. All the advertisement he did never worked. That day we took charge over that gate in that region. We subdued the Principality in charge in the Name of Jesus and commanded the gates to be opened to his business. The testimony is that within one year he opened another branch of that business. Glory be to the Lord. Most High.

Do you know how many people's lives and finances have been locked down in the marine kingdom and they wonder why things are not working for them? There are so many things that advance the people of God such as degrees, certificates, licenses which have not been granted or shut down by marine powers.

Church organizations are compromised and church leaders are bewildered all because they don't know how to deal with marine principalities. What you see in churches like that is lukewarm Christians and sexual promiscuity of all sorts, etc.

Decree today in the Name of Jesus and bind that marine principality controlling your life, holding you hostage. Release your destiny by fire in Jesus Name. In my book, *'Deliverance by Fire'* you will learn how to release missiles to every marine spirits.

CHAPTER TWO

SERPENTINE POWERS

I would like to share another stronghold of darkness. In the Garden of Eden, Satan possessed the serpent, (Gen. 3,) and ever since then, his demons have built their kingdoms around it, because of the nature of the serpent which is subtlety. The Bible most times refers to the Devil as the serpent. *"So the great dragon was cast out,* ***that serpent of old, called the Devil and Satan,*** *who deceives the whole world; he was cast to the earth, and his angels were cast out with him."* *Rev. 12:9*

The serpentine demons work hand in hand with the marine kingdom called the marine serpent. They possess similar qualities. The Bible also refers to it as the Leviathan. *"In that day the LORD* ***with His severe sword,*** *great and strong, Will punish Leviathan the fleeing serpent, Leviathan that twisted serpent; And He will slay the reptile that is in the sea."* Is. 27:1

This Principality is a strong and stubborn one. This one demon is the same one that really possessed Pharaoh in the Bible and wouldn't let the Israelites go. One of the emblems of Pharaoh's staff of power is that of a serpent.

He had it on his crown as well. It was one of the very first Principalities Moses had to deal with because he knew that it symbolized Pharaoh's strength and Power to dominate. Now, you will understand the reason why God had to turn Moses rod into a serpent.

> *Then the LORD spoke to Moses and Aaron, saying, "When Pharaoh speaks to you, saying, 'Show a miracle for yourselves,' then you shall say to Aaron,* **'Take your rod and cast it before Pharaoh, and let it become a serpent.'"** *So Moses and Aaron went in to Pharaoh, and they did so, just as the LORD commanded. And Aaron cast down his rod before Pharaoh and before his servants, and it became a serpent. But Pharaoh also called the wise men and the sorcerers; so the magicians of Egypt, they also did in like manner with their enchantments. For every man threw down his rod, and they became serpents.* **But Aaron's rod swallowed up their rods.** *And Pharaoh's heart grew hard, and he did not heed them, as the LORD had said.* Ex. 7:9-13

The Power of God swallowed up the rods of every evil Serpentine power, Hallelujah. Is there any power stronger than God? I don't think so. He created them all. He is the head of all so He knows how to deal with them.

> *For by Him all things were created that are in heaven and that are on earth, visible and invisible, whether **thrones or dominions or principalities** or powers. All things were created through Him and for Him.* Colossians 1:16

Again, Paul still made us understand the existence of these Principalities and made us understand that they can be subdued. That was what Moses did.

There are several signs or symptoms you see where a serpentine demon is at work. Most people who are possessed with this demon have one thing in common: "anger and stubbornness". When they are angry they don't see clearly anymore because the spirit blinds their natural eyes. This stubbornness always leads to destruction because of rage or anger. That was exactly what happened to Pharaoh: *"Then I will **harden** Pharaoh's heart, so that he will pursue them; and **I will gain honor** over Pharaoh and over all his army, that the Egyptians may know that I am the LORD,"* (Ex. 14:4). God allowed that Serpentine demon to push Pharaoh to his own destruction. When this demon takes over somebody or a family, you will always see anger, bitterness, and eventually destruction. They destroy and afterwards regret their actions because they are not sure what came over them. I can say this from a personal experience from my upbringing in our family, this Principality held us in bondage for a long time. Thank God for the Blood of Jesus.

Another sign of this demon at work is sexual promiscuity, (when a man or woman is unable to control their sexual desires). This demon is what is at work with most prostitutes and also men and women who cannot control their sexual desires. Another symptom is also having problems with lying. Even if a person who is under this spirit doesn't want to lie they end up doing so because they can't control themselves. Have you ever seen people who really know how to lie without thinking about it? Now, I am not just talking about lying your way out of trouble but an inability to simply speak the truth.

This demon has crept into many churches today. The falsehood including false prophecies you hear in the Body of Christ is caused by this demon. Many who flow in the prophetic gift or ministry really have to watch out for this serpent spirit. They are subtle and like to pollute the anointing.

Also, this demon manifests in homosexuals as well. Serpents like to crawl over themselves each other just like homosexuals like to caress themselves each other with the affection that supposedly should be between a man and woman. That was God's original intent.

This Demon manifests itself in deceit, craftiness, etc. Most people who have this issue sometimes see snakes in their dreams, or sometime feel as though there is a snake around them when they are by themselves; they can actually feel it. This demon can also become a monitoring serpent that follows people everywhere. There are some voodoo priests who like to send this demon to undertake assignments on their behalf. They are sent to sabotage good things, and frustrates people's mission.

The Name and Blood of Jesus are strong forces, able to demolish the Power of darkness. Please pray right now against the Serpentine powers contending against you… subdue it in Jesus Name. Chase them out of your gates by the fire of the Holy Ghost.

CHAPTER THREE

WITCHCRAFT KINGDOM

The Principality of the Air is in charge of witchcraft activity in a region. This is another ancient kingdom that needs to be subdued for the glory of God to be manifested. Witchcraft practice is an ancient practice found in the Bible. Sometimes the Bible uses words like Sorcery or Medium to describe witchcraft activity. Most ancient religions from the Egyptian to the Babylonian religion in the Old Testament practiced witchcraft. Witchcraft was a big and respected profession in the Old Testament days. They were referred to as Magicians, Sorcerers, Enchanters, etc. Most Rulers and Kings had these Magicians or Sorcerers as part of their kingdom because the practice of divination was the order of the day. This was all part of Satan's deception to infiltrate God's plan for mankind. God had to literally forbid this practice from the children of Israel as He formed them into a people and a nation. It was part of the Laws they were given to the children of Israel.

*There shall not be found among you anyone who makes his son or his daughter pass through the fire, or one who practices **witchcraft**, or a soothsayer, or one who interprets omens, or a **sorcerer**, or one who conjures spells, or a **medium**, or a **spiritist**, or one who calls up the dead. For all who do these things are an abomination to the LORD, and because of these abominations the LORD your God drives them out from before you.* Deut. 18:10-12

Jezebel was also another Sorceress who was a witch in Israel. She was demonized and possessed and as such had manipulative powers to control people's destinies. She held the peace of the nation in her hand: *"Now it happened, when Joram saw Jehu, that he said, "Is it peace, Jehu? So he answered, "**What peace**, as long as the harlotries of your mother Jezebel and **her witchcraft are so many**?"* 2 Kings 9:22.

Do you see how the witchcraft powers can distort the lives of many if not subdued? Elijah contended against this kingdom in his days. Jezebel fought Elijah's ministry but he was victorious and was used to liberate God's people from bondage, (1 Kings 19). It was a battle. Elijah represented the Kingdom of God while Jezebel represented the Witchcraft Kingdom. If you don't put these wicked powers where they belong all you'll experience is darkness. Demons of witchcraft are known as wicked spirits. They are the powers of darkness. They love to see people suffer. They also project curses and enchantment on people, over a region or city but the real purpose of these evil spirits is destruction. Wherever you see lots of bloodshed, homicide, killings of all sorts you know the spirit of witchcraft is at work. When these demons possesses people you see evil attributes at work in them like destructions, killings, spreading evil rumor against people, destroying people's image or career, conspiracy and poverty. These demons are primarily responsible for poverty in a place or people. I am yet to see a poverty stricken place on earth where you don't see witchcraft practice in motion. In some places they have a warlock that acts as the principality of the community. The wealth of the people has been transferred to the kingdom of darkness. So one of the ways to release people into the prosperity which God has for them is to destroy every witchcraft altar and coven existing in their lives just like Elijah did in 1 Kings 18. Please read my other book: *'Deliverance by Fire'* for the prayer guide against witchcraft powers.

There is a thin line between the Prophetic ministry and Witchcraft.

Now that you know how this kingdom operates, you cannot give them an inch. They are nothing but wicked spirits. These demons have not only succeeded in destroying people's lives but have crept into the church as well. These demons have possessed some ministers of the gospel. I am yet to see a Prophetic ministry that does not attract the Jezebel spirit. This is the spirit of witchcraft, control, manipulations, etc. Where there is a Power oriented ministry, these demons like to try and test the minister of such a ministry. *There is a thin line between the Prophetic ministry and Witchcraft.* Both of them have to do with Power demonstration. The Prophetic is Godly influence, while Witchcraft is satanic influence. The only thing that keeps the Prophet from delving into witchcraft is when they operate in an understanding of the Word of God. It guides and protects when the Prophet penetrates the spirit realm.

CHAPTER FOUR

OCCULT POWERS IN HIGH PLACES

This chapter is very crucial to understanding the end time revival that must take place in the Western world because this revival will ultimately bring restoration to the Church at large. We are living in a time where the church is so confused concerning what exactly is going on in our societies especially when it comes to spiritual and religious influence.

High Places are normally places of power and influence. When the Bible speaks of High Places, it means position of authority and influence over a people. Whoever is in the High Places, they control the people. I have said it previously and I will reiterate this point again; whatever demons are in Power, that is the demon that controls the people.

Now you will understand why Saul had to be exalted to the High Place of influence to sit with honorable people before his ordination. He had to feel what it meant to be in power and to be influential. You can call it a rite of passage if you would.

Samuel answered Saul and said, "I am the seer. Go up before me to the high place, for you shall eat with me today; and tomorrow I will let you go and will tell you all that is in your heart. But as for your donkeys that were lost three days ago, do not be anxious about them, for they have been found. And on whom is all the desire of Israel? Is it not on you and on all your father's house?" And Saul answered and said, "Am I not a Benjamite, of the smallest of the tribes of Israel, and my family the least of all the families of the tribe of Benjamin? Why then do you speak like this to me?" Now Samuel took Saul and his servant and brought them into the hall, and had them sit in the place of honor among those who were invited; there were about thirty persons. And Samuel said to the cook, "Bring the portion which I gave you, of which I said to you, 'Set it apart.'" So the cook took up the thigh with its upper part and set it before Saul. And Samuel said, "Here it is, what was kept back. It was set apart for you. Eat; for until this time it has been kept for you, since I said I invited the people." So Saul ate with Samuel that day. When they had come down from the high

place into the city, Samuel spoke with Saul on the
top of the house. 1 Sam. 9:19-25

In America there are occult powers that have
infiltrated the High Places of authority and influence. These
powers operate in people who are decision makers - they
control the government; economy; education; politics, and
also have infiltrated into the church. That is one reason why
it looks as if the church is not making the impact it should.
Please understand that it is not because there is no more
Power in the Body of Christ but it's because we've not
taught our people the art of strategic spiritual warfare or the
devices of the enemy. Christians don't know how to tackle
these demonic powers in the High Places. We have those in
public offices strategically positioned by God for His
kingdom sake like Joseph in Egypt and Daniel in Babylon
and Esther in Babylon as well. If they don't know why they
are there or know how to counteract demonic forces they
will defeat the purpose of God in their lives.

You can hardly get into a notable position in this
country without going through these demonic forces. They
are everywhere of influence from the media to the White
House and everywhere in-between. If you want to be heard
and taken seriously then get ready to fight these forces of

darkness. They promote satanic agendas that contradict the Christian Faith.

There two key occult powers in High Places today that every Christian ought to know about: *'Freemasonry Fraternity and the New Age Religion'*.

These two occult groups have become so influential in America because their way of operation is subtle and manipulative which of course is the Devil's strategy. You begin to experience their presence from college all the way to the employment office and then to the High Places of society. The average graduate has to experience a greater influence; one which comes from God. We need to pray that once our children have graduated, that they will become involved in church activities that are in place to recharge and revitalize their faith because while they were in school their minds have been injected by all kinds of indoctrination under the auspices of intellectualism from many occult professors. Some professors and school administrators are nothing more than recruiters for some modern day cults we see in operation today. Therefore, we have to understand the times that we are living in and comprehend that our educated youth have endured so much demonic bombardment, all in the notion or name of attaining educational success.

The Freemasonry society is one of the most influential occult in the Western world that is believed to have been in existence since 1390. This fraternal organization promotes a satanic agenda of a one world government which will eventually prepare the world for the anti-Christ. It is also believed that every Prime Minister in Britain from the first 'prime minister,' Robert Walpole (1676-1745), to Ramsey MacDonald (1866–1937,) was a Grand Master; a pattern that is replicated throughout the world under the influence of Freemasonry. Therefore, it is no surprise to find that every U. S. President until John F Kennedy (1917–63) was a high degree Freemason. The Freemasonic denomination of power is pervasive within the societies it functions and percolates down from the highest level. All power structures within the western world, such as the judiciary, the police, the armed forces and the civil service, are *ensnared in a web of corruption.* The Power structure of America is confined within the parameters of the Masonic cult. It is no wonder why it is more of spiritual warfare for any Christian who decides to penetrate the structure of government and politics in this Country. Freemasonry is a cult within a cult with an organized system of governance. It is an all inclusive religion. Does this sound familiar? Genesis 11, (the Tower of Babel,) typifies this one world government. This is the democracy we see today in America because the Constitution of America was written by the founding fathers that were part of the Freemasonry organization. So you see people who are involved in all kinds of demonic religions, who are positioned in governmental places of power like the United Nations which is the central distribution office of the Masonic organization; promoting the one world government for the anti-Christ system. They have succeeded in building this system in such a way that accommodates all religions including Christianity but most Christians are so naïve to the spiritual implications or warfare involved. Since the Christian allegiance represents the Kingdom of Light, spiritually they should be a major threat to the kingdom of darkness. However, most times these Christians are either forced to compromise their faith because their views are not popular. If they go against what is popular; they may jeopardized their employment.

Daniel went through the same attack in the workplace, but he chose not to compromise his faith.

Then this Daniel distinguished himself above the governors and satraps, because an excellent spirit was in him; and the king gave thought to setting him over the whole realm. So the governors and satraps sought to find some charge against Daniel concerning the kingdom; but they could find no charge or fault, because he was faithful; nor was there any error or fault found in him. Then these men said, "We shall not find any charge against this Daniel unless we find it against him concerning the law of his God. Dan. 6:3-5

You see the reason why you as a Christian in the white collar sector must be very prayerful in order to excel. The Freemasonry Cult protects itself in numerous ways. They use code phrases such as, "Are you on the level?" Also, they use secret handshakes and gestures. Furthermore, this organization is even more serious in its dealings with its enemies and betrayers. Some are murdered or assassinated while others, more often, suffer career termination, financial and social ostracism, judicial corruption, blackmail and scandalous set-ups. The "charity" of Freemasonry is indeed a strange brew, indeed.

It is time for Christians to pray for our nation. Let the revival fires burn from the Oval office of the White House to the media so that the good news of the Kingdom can be heralded throughout our land. We need to pray for the Daniels and Josephs in our societies who are strategically positioned to unleash the Kingdom of God in each sphere of influence they are called to function in.

The New Age religion on the other hand masks itself with the search of inner truth or self discovery. It promotes one's self image as god rather than promoting the Power of God within mankind. So we don't really need any God anywhere if we can discover the power within ourselves. Seekers of truth outside the Bible often fall prey to this satanic agenda of not needing God because you are god on your own if only you can develop the innermost part of your being. See what the Bible says:

"I said, "You are gods, And all of you are children of the Most High." Psalm 82:6.

We are only gods on earth because we are first children of the God of Heaven. So our strength, power, authority comes from God above. Outside of Him we are nothing. This is true Christianity, but the New Age teaches we are god on our own without the God of Heaven. Again, it promotes total liberation, freewill with no boundaries whatsoever. Trust me; this is what people want to hear today. Nevertheless, God already created us as free moral beings with our free will. This free will for the Christian is within the parameter of the overall will of God for us. This New Age religion is growing tremendously, capturing the elite and the young generation of today because of its mask under rights and freedom your own way, your own taste and your own opinion – that's all that matters. It is satanic to be rebellious against God and His will for us.

> **We need deliverance; we have practiced polytheism long enough.**

In America, the average child rebel against their parents and 'the disconnect' is not only in the home; it can also be found at school. I believe this onslaught of rebellion is taking place because our children are being taught to be tolerant and accept all religions, all people; gay or straight, it doesn't matter - all roads lead to God. We need deliverance; *we have practiced polytheism long enough.* The future of our children is as stake. Where are the Daniels and the Josephs of our generation? You must not be carried away; you must not grow weary and please do not bow to any evil idol in the workplace. Would you pray right now that God will use you as an agent of change in the marketplace and in the workplace in Jesus Name. Begin to possess the gates in the workplace. You are in charge where you work. Until you take your rightful place at the gate, the Devil will continue his mess. Joseph was a slave in Portiphar's house yet he was in charge of the gate spiritually. *"So it was, from the time that he had made him overseer of his house and all that he had, that the LORD blessed the Egyptian's house for Joseph's sake; and the blessing of the LORD was on all that he had in the house and in the field."* Gen. 39:5

There is a reason why you are positioned where you are; God wants to use you. You must not keep silent; you are the deliverer the world is waiting for. *"For if you remain completely silent at this time, relief and deliverance will arise for the Jews from another place, but you and your father's house will perish.* ***Yet who knows whether you have come to the kingdom for such a time as this."*** Esther 4:14

Start by possessing the gate and chase out every demonic forces assigned to control your office. Take charge in Jesus Name.

"Those who do wickedly against the covenant he shall corrupt with flattery; ***but the people who know their God shall be strong, and carry out great exploits."*** Dan. 11:32

PART FOUR

LET THE CHURCH ARISE

INTRODUCTION

This book has been very enlightening to me as the author. I hope that I have inspired many to see and understand the importance of spiritual warfare in the Kingdom of God.

> *God is not coming for a defeated, 'save me, I am dying,' kind of church.*

The Church has a major role to play in the end time revival, the end time restoration and reformation being birth in the earth. We are about to see an unusual move of the Holy Spirit upon the earth. Nations, cities and regions will experience the latter rain glory that has been prophesied over the ages. The Body of Christ has a major role to play in this revival. The church must be ready for the harvest. Therefore, the last part of this intriguing book will focus on what the church must do in order to partner with God in His agenda of the restoration project that is already in motion. *God is not coming for a defeated, save me I am dying kind of church.* Jesus Christ did not prophesy of a defeated church. He is coming for a triumphant and victorious church which is called to reign on the earth. We are to possess the earth and represent God here. *"Your kingdom come. Your will be done on earth as it is in heaven."* Matt. 6:10

CHAPTER ONE

I WILL BUILD MY CHURCH

*When Jesus came into the **region of Caesarea Philippi**, He asked His disciples, saying, "Who do men say that I, the Son of Man, am?" So they said, "Some say John the Baptist, some Elijah, and others Jeremiah or one of the prophets." He said to them, "But who do you say that I am?"Simon Peter answered and said, "**You are the Christ, the Son of the living God.**" Jesus answered and said to him, "Blessed are you, Simon Bar-Jonah, for flesh and blood has not revealed this to you, but My Father who is in heaven. And I also say to you that you are Peter, and **on this rock I will build My church**, and **the gates of Hades shall not prevail against it.** And **I will give you the keys of the kingdom of heaven**, and whatever you bind on earth will be bound in heaven, and whatever you loose on earth will be loosed in heaven."* Matt. 16:13-19

When Jesus and His disciples got to the region of Caesarea Philippi, He stopped and from that day the Church was released in the Spirit awaiting manifestation in the natural. What is it about Caesarea Philippi? Let's see the historical background of this place:

Caesarea Philippi is one of the most pleasant sites in Israel -- it is on a terrace 1,150 feet high overlooking a fertile valley. It is also an area scattered with the temples of ancient Syrian Baal worship. Historians have listed at least fourteen such temples -- it was a place beneath the shadow of ancient gods. There are several references to this area in the Old Testament. The northernmost conquest of Joshua is described as ranging from "the mountains of Israel and its lowlands, from Mount Halak and the ascent to Seir, even as far as Baal Gad in the Valley of Lebanon below Mount Hermon" (Joshua 11:17). A cave near Caesarea Philippi is said to be the birthplace of the Greek god Pan, the god of nature, fields, forests, mountains, flocks and shepherds. "He is son of Hermes by one or another nymph; his mother was so scared by his appearance that she abandoned him at birth and Hermes introduced him to Olympus. His name is probably related to the same root as Latin pasco, and thus means 'shepherd.'" (Richard Stoneman, Greek Mythology, p. 136). The cult of Pan originated in Arcadia, a pastoral region in Greece. Greek travelers, finding the landscape was like their homeland, established this area of worship to Pan. During the Hellenistic period, a sanctuary was built to Pan. There are five niches hewn out of rock to the right of the cave -- at one time they probably held statues -- three of the niches bear inscriptions in Greek mentioning Pan, Echo and Galerius (one of Pan's priests). The original name for Caesarea Philippi was Panias (also spelt Paneas, Paneion and Paneias). The modern name is Banias -- an Arabic corruption of Panias. The Jordan river has four main sources, and the cave at Caesarea Philippi is its' easternmost source -- this alone would make the area full of emotion for the Jews. In Caesarea Philippi there was a great temple of white marble built to the godhead of Caesar -- it had been built by Herod the Great. "At Paneas Antiochius III defeated the Ptolemies of Egypt in 200 BCE, thus establishing Seleucid rule in Palestine and Syria In 20 BCE, Augustus gave Paneas to King Herod who erected there a temple of white marble to his patron (Josephus, Antiq. 15, 10.3/360); but the city was built only later by his son Herod Philip. In 2 B.C. Herod the Great's son, Philip, named it Caesarea in honor of Augustus, and, to differentiate it from Caesarea Maritima, it became known as Caesarea Philippi. Later, Herod Agrippa would call the place Neroneas in honor of the Emperor Nero. After the destruction of Jerusalem, "The victors gave no quarter, but slew all Jews upon whom they could lay their hands; 97,000 fugitives were caught and sold as slaves; many of them died as unwilling gladiators in the triumphal games that were celebrated at Berytus, Caesarea Philippi and Rome." (Will Durant, Caesar And Christ, p. 545).[6]

Jesus stopped here on purpose. This place happened to be a major stronghold of darkness like we have read from history. It was time to take over the gates and the city. Jesus asked the question to see if His disciples truly knew what His mission was. Simon responded by the Spirit. The prophetic declaration of Jesus is where the Church of today needs to be.

Jesus changed Simon's name, hitherto, his destiny changed as well. In Bible times, names reflected destiny. He said Peter's destiny had to be changed to conform to his mission. Now the prophetic nature of the Church of Jesus Christ was revealed: *"Upon this **rock** I will build my **church** and the **gates of Hades** shall not prevail against it."* There are 3 profound revelations in this verse that must be explained.

1. **Rock:** This means Jesus the Rock of Ages. He has been here before the very beginning. He is the Ancient of Days, the Beginning and the End. Upon this recognition, acknowledgement and acceptance of this revelation the Church is laid on a solid foundation that cannot be uprooted. The Rock is the foundation of our Christianity. Jesus who is the Rock is also the Chief Cornerstone of the Church which shall stand forever!

2. **Church:** The word *church* is a Greek term *'ekklessia' which means 'Called Out'*. It was a political term which applied to an *assembly of citizens* "called-out" for a particular purpose. In the Greco-Roman world, the elders of the city normally had meetings to discuss business or agendas of their city. All free citizens of the city-state were summoned to these regular assemblies where decisions of government were made by a majority vote.

A person described as *ekkletos* was someone selected to judge or render a decision. Xenophon, the ancient Greek historian, describes a group called on to render a decision about the requests of some ambassadors during a time of civil war. He describes this group as ekkletos. In like manner, an ekklesia was summoned because decisions or judgments had to be made. [7]

Jesus declared that He would build His Church. The idea is that He would call out a group of people, (Christians) who would become citizens of the Kingdom of God He came to inaugurate on earth. That was why He said no one can come, see or enter the Kingdom, except he is 'born again,' (John 3:3-5). So the entrance to the Kingdom of God was Christ himself.

After becoming citizens of the Kingdom of God, then you are called out from the rest of the world: *Therefore Come out from among them and be separate, says the Lord. Do not touch what is unclean, and I will receive you." I will be a Father to you, and you shall be my sons and daughters, says the LORD Almighty."* II Cor. 6:17-18

Now, after becoming a citizen of Christ's Kingdom, you are the *'Church;'* an assembly of God's people who make decision on what happens on earth. You are in charge. This is the beginning of authority.

> ***Jesus declared concerning the Church: "the gates of Hades shall not prevail against it."***

3. **Gates of Hades:** Remember, we have learnt so much about gates. Gates represent dominion, authority, power, and influence. These characteristics are kingdom features. Whoever controls the gate controls the people.

Hades refers to Hell. Hell is a present place of torment where lost souls go to; awaiting final judgment. While believers pass and go to paradise, lost souls are locked in Hades. It is a kingdom of darkness. Satan and his Demons are in charge in this place. This was where Jesus Christ descended into to take back the key that was once lost and also free the souls that had been imprisoned there. (Matt. 27:52-53 and Rev. 1:18)

So Jesus declared concerning the Church: *"the gates of Hades shall not prevail against it."* This means that no matter how much the Kingdom of Hell try to pull the people of God into their Kingdom for destruction; they will not be successful. Jesus came to inaugurate His Kingdom of Light to deliver many from the eternal destruction and oppression of the Devil. So the Church becomes those that have been called out of destruction and torment. The Church becomes the arm of the Kingdom of God that is stretched out to deliver many who receive Jesus Christ. The Church is militant in nature to repossess what Satan has stolen. We are to take back destinies, cities and nations. *The Church, therefore, is an offensive Church not a defensive one.* As we possess territories, Jesus declares we cannot be stopped by the Powers of Darkness. He means we are too loaded to be grounded, we must continue to advance God's Kingdom, and de-populate Hell. This is our commission. What we see today is the church playing defensive tactics because many lack understanding. When we do this, we endanger the lives of people. Satan is a wicked being, he has no mercy. He knows he is doomed and he wants to take as many as he can with him. Let the Church arise and bring deliverance to this generation.

CHAPTER TWO

THE AUTHORITY OF THE CHURCH

One chapter is not enough to explore on this subject of Church Authority which is also the Believer's Authority. It is a vast one that requires its own book. I will streamline this teaching and in so doing, attempt not to digress off the overall subject matter.

Understanding the Authority of the Church is to delve into the Power available to us as Believers. It's all connected to the Scripture from the last chapter:

*And I also say to you that you are Peter, and on this rock I will build My church, and the gates of Hades shall not prevail against it. And **I will give you the keys of the kingdom of heaven, and whatever you bind on earth will be bound in heaven, and whatever you loose on earth will be loosed in heaven.** "* Matt. 16:18-19

Once again, the owner of the Church, the King of the Kingdom, declares that He (Jesus,) will give those He called out (the Church,) keys of the Kingdom of Heaven.

Keys represent authority. It means that whatever that happens in Heaven can be done on earth. The Church is called to reproduce Heaven on earth.

Jesus said with this authority He has given the Church that whatever we bind and loose on earth will be honored in Heaven. So, whatever we allow is allowed and whatever we disallow is disallowed. The destiny of every generation is in the hands of the church. We must take it very serious. The same Devil that is tormenting the world, we must remember was cast out of Heaven:

> *And war broke out in heaven: Michael and his angels fought with the dragon; and the dragon and his angels fought, but **they did not prevail, nor was a place found for them in heaven any longer.** So **the great dragon was cast out, that serpent of old, called the Devil and Satan, who deceives the whole world; he was cast to the earth, and his angels were cast out with him.*** Rev. 12:7-9

The same authority that was displayed in Heaven has been passed unto the Church. We can cast the Old Devil and His Demons out of regions, out of systems and out of people. The truth is wherever there is a Church the

Devil must have no place to operate there. The Church is in charge of that gate. We addressed the idea of the word *'Church'* in the last chapter. It is clear that we decide what happens in the places we reside. The government is in control physically but we are in charge spiritually. Whatever you see happening today has its root in the spirit realm. Whoever is in charge spiritually is the real boss. I am happy to announce that as a Christian I am in charge of my destiny; as the Church, we are in charge of the city and as the Body of Christ, we are in charge of the nation. It is time to start exercising our authority. It is possible to have keys and still be locked out of the house if you don't use them. The Church has been locked out from what is rightfully hers for some time. I decree it is time to come out and take your rightful place in this generation in Jesus Name.

> *While we are waiting on God,*
> *God is waiting on us.*

Let the Church arise and let her enemies be scattered. Let the church arise and let the Devil flee. Let the Church arise and let the Kingdom citizens begin to possess the land in Jesus Name. Anytime the Church arises in unity to repossess what is rightfully hers; Heaven must respond. It happened in the early church:

> *Peter was therefore kept in prison,* **but constant** **prayer was offered to God for him by the church.** *And when Herod was about to bring him out, that night Peter was sleeping, bound with two chains between two soldiers; and the guards before the door were keeping the prison. Now behold, an angel of the Lord stood by him, and a light shone in the prison; and he struck Peter on the side and raised him up, saying, "Arise quickly!" And his chains fell off his hands. Then the angel said to him, "Gird yourself and tie on your sandals"; and so he did. And he said to him, "Put on your garment and follow me." So he went out and followed him, and did not know that what was done by the angel was real, but thought he was seeing a vision. When they were past the first and the second guard posts, they came to the iron gate that leads to the city, which opened to them of its own accord; and they went out and went down one street, and immediately the angel departed from him.* **And when Peter had** **come to himself, he said, "Now I know for certain** **that the Lord has sent His angel, and has delivered**

me from the hand of Herod and from all the expectation of the Jewish people. Acts 12:5-11

The story of Peter in prison is a type of where the Church is today. Peter represents destinies locked up in Demonic prisons. It was when the Church rose up in prayers that Heaven responded. Constant prayers were made. It was a consistent effort to see breakthrough happen. People are bound in prison chains of darkness crying for deliverance. Only if the Church will get back on her purpose again to possess the gates of the enemy we will see the revival that we all desire.

While we are waiting on God, God is waiting on us. We are asking where is the God of Elijah? God is asking where is the Elijah of God? Let's us start confronting the Kingdom of Darkness rather than tolerating it. Let's put the Devil where he belongs. You must know with all certainty that Power and Might belongs to the Lord forever and ever! Amen.

Other Books By Author

Journey Of Faith

Prayer That Touches Heaven

Dr. George Agbonson

Prayer That Touches Heaven

JOURNEY of FAITH

DR. GEORGE AGBONSON

Destined For Greatness

Transformational Leadership

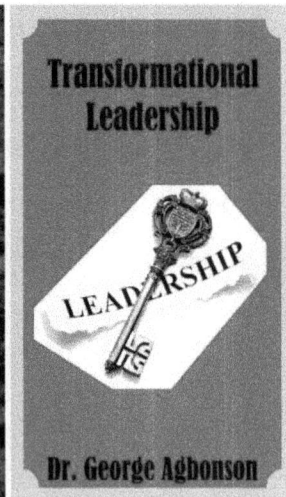

Destined For Greatness

Transformational Leadership

LEADERSHIP

Dr. George Agbonson

Dr. George Agbonson

Deliverance By Fire

Releasing Prayer Missiles

Apostle George Agbonson

CONTACT:

Christ Restoration Ministries International

U.S.A

Head Office:

740 Lakeview Plaza Blvd. Unit 325

Worthington, OH 43085

TEL: 614-307-3297

www.christrestoration.net

Email: admin@christrestoration.net

BIBLIOGRAPHY

1. Frangipane Francis, *The Three Battlegrounds.* Cedar Rapids, Arrow Publications, Inc. 2006

2. Fernandez Manny, *In Drug Fight on Texas Border Some Officers Play both sides.* www.nytimes.com, January 2, 2013

3. Ibid. 1

4. Unpublished Work: *Possess the gates*, Jane Vaughn January 2006

5. Rhoel Lomahan, *Building at the Gates-Nehemiah 3:1-32* 23. www.westloop-church.org, November 2009

6. David Padfield, *Caesarea Philippi In Israel.* www.padfield.com

7. Glenn Kerr, *Ekklessia Its Form and Function.* www.hallmarkbaptist.com